A View From The Stands

A Season with Bob the Beerman

By Bob D. Beerman
as told to
Bob Donchez

A View from the Stands - A Season with Bob the Beerman
by Bob D. Beerman as told to Bob Donchez

Copyright © 1994 by Bob D. Beerman and Bob Donchez

Published by Successful Concepts
P. O. Box 3266 Boulder, CO 80307-3266
(303) 499-5926
(800) FULL-MUG
(800) 385-5684

Direct inquiries and/or orders to the above address.

Sale of this book without a front cover may be unauthorized. If this book is coverless, it may have been reported to the publisher as "unsold or destroyed" and neither the authors nor the publisher may have received payment for it.

Publisher's Note: Many of the products and services mentioned in these pieces are trademarks of their respective companies. Every effort has been made to identify these trademarks by initial capitalization. Should there be an omission in this respect, we shall be pleased to make the necessary corrections in future printings.

All rights reserved. Except for use in a review, no portion of this book may be reproduced in any form without the express written permission of the publisher.

ISBN: 0-9640341-0-7

Library of Congress Catalog Card Number: 94-65390

Cover illustration by Lueb Popoff - Hollow Log

Design by Dave Stevens, Stevens & Associates Marketing & Communications Services

Back cover photo by Wendy Rubin with technical assistance from David Barwin

Manufactured in the United States of America

Forward

Wall Streeter by day, Beerman by night! As the rusted steel batting cage is rolled out for the first time each spring, Bob Donchez steps into a nearby dugout and becomes . . . Bob the Beerman. Or does he?
And so the legend was born.
A former Master of the Universe for Salomon Brothers in Gotham, New York City, Bob sought truth, justice, and to be Master of His Own Life.
Playing with millions of dollars of other people's money, Bob noticed the co-workers around him. For rich people, they didn't look very happy. And deep inside, neither was Bob.
So he packed his MBA into his creative suitcase and departed Metropolis, leaving behind the best and worst of both worlds. Fine dining and fine friends, Broadway and bagels, the Metropolitan Opera and the Metropolitan Museum. And crime and crack, drugs and drunks, homeless and helpless.
Even a man of steel suspenders and a bullet-proof ego needed some fresh breezes and open spaces. Though he was capable of bringing a fleet of commuter buses to a dead halt by leveraging the company's stock, Bob wasn't capable of consuming clean air when running alongside the 5:45 crosstown local.
Fun became foreign. But fear was never a factor, other than the fear of not contributing to "Duty and Humanity." Realizing life's short and it's never certain when the last call would come, he left the Big Apple in search of fun, service, and adventure.
With that, he enjoys life, is kind to others, and gives something back to mankind.
"Look, up in the stands! It's a bird! It's a plane! It's Bob the Beerman!"
The legend lives!

For our friends and families, both immediate and extended, and the fans in the stands. And especially for all those who laugh at themselves on a regular basis.

Special thanks to Michael, K. Hawkeye, Todd, Dave, and Larry. And also to Dave, Andy, Art, Erma, David, and Jerry.

INTRODUCTION

Write what you know about.
  Mark Twain

Baseball is a billion-dollar industry. Both authors of this book operate on a shoe-string budget. Ballplayers sign contracts averaging in excess of one million dollars a year. The authors had difficulty finding anyone willing to offer a publishing contract.

It's been said baseball officials have lost touch with their market, the fans. The authors know their market well, having spent a season serving baseball's spectators.

Baseball is entertainment. The co-authors are performers at heart.

Baseball news is found in the sports pages, the business pages, and the front pages. The authors wrote tabloid sports, worked in big business, and stayed off the front pages.

The Giants and the Dodgers once played in New York. Then they left.

Both authors lived and played in New York. Then they left.

Ballplayers give up their big league careers for endorsement deals. The co-authors gave up corporate careers to write this book.

Baseball is a kid's game. Both authors still play games and don't know what they want to do when they grow up. Except, have *A View from the Stands*.

TABLE OF CONTENTS

Ballpark Sensations	1
Parking	4
Tickets Please	8
Guys Are Different Than Women	14
Ballpark Sounds	16
Hot Air	20
The Grand Island Gang	22
Family Section	25
Remember Me, I Saw You Opening Day	29
Ballpark Economics	31
The Opposite Sex	35
Away Games	38
Celebrity Row	42
I Want You To Buy That Person A Beer	47
What About Bob?	50
Lean, Mean, Fighting Machines	53
Fickle Fans' Bill Of Rights	56
Foot Power	60
What Do You Do In Real Life?	64
Stadium Social Status	68
What I Really Meant Was . . .	72
Freebies, Promotions, And Giveaways	76
Rest Rooms	81
High Pressure Sales Pitches	84
Businessperson's Special	88
Financial Markets and Ballplayers	92
Health-Conscious Approach to Baseball	95
Radio Daze	98
Baseball Strategy	101

No Drinking And Driving	104
Press Conference Language	106
Let's Play Two	110
Yesterday's Duds	114
Learning To Score	118
Stretching	121
Armchair Guide To Televised Baseball	123
So, You Wanted To Be A Beerman?	126
Where Can I Get Some . . .	129
Realignment	132
Malfunctions	134
The End Of A Love Affair	136

BALLPARK SENSATIONS

A beautiful game, superbly played. . . . Yes, a grand game, a game entirely worthy of its reputation.
> Arnold Bennett, the British writer's reaction to seeing his first baseball game, 1912

Opening Day at Mile High Stadium with the expansion Colorado Rockies brought back memories of the first ball game I attended with my father. Small pleasures and simple thoughts experienced that one special summer evening, when I took the initial rites of manhood and saw my first major league game, were allowed to surface under the backdrop of an April sun set proud in the white-blue sky. On this day of the Rockies' home debut, a new generation of fathers and their sons would make the passage to baseball buddies. An entire population of Rocky Mountain men would be baptized to a virgin rite of spring.

The joy brought to these families by the inaugural journey to a big league game made me recall some of my first ballpark memories:
- The hustle and bustle of the crowd moving en masse toward the stadium.
- The anticipation at the ticket window, as you wondered if you'd be able to purchase tickets close enough to the field to obtain a player's autograph.
- Passing through the turnstiles and seeing the hawkers peddling their wares.
- Buying a yearbook and scorecard, so Dad could teach you to keep score.

A View from the Stands

- The aroma of the hot dogs, popcorn, and fresh-roasted peanuts as you walked up the ramp toward the seats.
- The deep reverence upon walking through a darkened tunnel, toward the light of day, and then suddenly opening onto the panoramic view of the freshly cut field trimmed with the white icing marking the foul lines and batter's box.
- The subtle disappointment upon reaching your seats and realizing that they were almost at the top of the stadium. But this was offset by the hope that you would still get a foul ball. Just in case, you kept your Spalding baseball mitt poised on your hand in the ready position until an usher came by in the second inning and told you that no ball had ever been hit into this level of the ballpark.
- The excitement, when, two batters after the usher had left, a towering fly ball is lifted high into the coal-black sky and above your seat level, a sure-to-be home run. Then the dashed hopes when the shortstop squeezes the ball in his glove for the last out of the inning. You never realized how difficult it is to judge a batted ball when sitting so high in the stands. It's then that your father instructs you to watch the fielders' movements on balls hit in the air. The one looking up at it will be the one to catch it.
- How it didn't matter that your favorite team, the worst in baseball, was playing the second worst.
- Your dad flagging down a passing hot dog vendor, getting two with mustard, then buying two Cokes from the soda man. And the taste of the hot dog was the best you've ever had in your short life. You still savor the flavor, even though the dog was barely boiled and the bun was as soggy as the afternoon newspaper in a summer rainstorm.
- Checking the out-of-town scoreboard every inning to see if your team gained any ground on all those ahead of it in the standings.
- The tempered excitement of seeing, in person, your first big league home run, even if it was hit by the opposing team.
- Flipping through the yearbook between innings in search of the glossy-colored action pictures of your favorite players, and deciding where in your bedroom to hang the fold-out composite team picture.
- Your dad showing how to crack a peanut shell and peel the skin

from the nut, then handing you a couple to try. Once shelling a few successfully, reaching into your dad's crumpled brown paper bag and pulling out a handful of peanuts for yourself. You no longer required dad's guidance.
-Studying the player stats from the scorecard and concluding with youthful exuberance that next year your team could contend for the pennant, despite being forty-six games out on this early August day.
-Your dad explaining the difference between a slider and a curve ball, then you trying to determine what type the last pitch was - from the nosebleed seats.
-The jubilation when your team hits a home run to put it ahead by one run late in the contest.
-The muted dejection when your team fails to hold a ninth inning lead and loses the game. But your dad buffers this with the purchase of a team pennant for you while leaving the stadium.
-After the game, relief that your dad remembers where the family station wagon is located in the labyrinth-like parking area because you are too tired to spend time searching for it in case he forgot.
-Falling asleep a few minutes into the ride home and dreaming about the baseball memories of a lifetime and vanquishing those of the loss.

A View from the Stands

PARKING

By the end of the season, I feel like a used car.
   Journeyman catcher Bob Brenly

Ever wonder why municipalities are so anxious to construct stadiums? It's because some politician with a high-level window office desires to leave a legacy for his citizenry. Better to desire this than the secretary down the hall, I guess. So, he pushes through a bond issue to finance the construction of a monument to himself.

Then he solicits other cities' professional sports teams. He wines and dines these big league owners and offers tax incentives and sweetheart deals. Then he prays that a team will be relocated to his new stadium by one of these owners with bags of money.

That's kind of redundant, isn't it? After all, you or I, an average working stiff, don't own a major league team.

By finding a tenant for his yet to be completed coliseum, Mr. Elected Official can become even more big and powerful and run for a higher office and move out of town to some place like Washington, D.C.

One slight problem. Your friendly politician - yes, the one you voted into office for the last 13 terms - enticed Mr. Big League Owner with so many carrots that the vegetable garden is bare.

Let's see. The local politician gave the new team in town the use of a rent-free stadium, seventy-five percent of concession revenue, fifty percent of parking income, and twenty-five percent of all the best parking spots at every shopping mall in a fifty-mile radius.

So what does your friendly politician do? Remember, you

voted for him, and so did your parents, and their parents.

He passes a usage tax and a ticket surcharge. Now, if anyone knows what a usage tax is, please let me know. Will I be taxed for using a personal computer to write this silly book? If I use my toilet, will I be forced to dump some of my hard-earned money back to the city? Or is each flush covered by the water tax?

And what about a ticket surcharge? Once upon a time, you could walk up to a ticket window two hours before a game or show and buy a pair of seats. Try that now. How about phoning the stadium or arena to purchase tickets? It used to be you could dial the stadium ticket office directly, buy a couple of tickets, and have them waiting at the will call window.

Now, you want a couple of tickets for the ball game? Does the team sell them in advance? For nine out of ten events, you must go through some third-party ticket agency, like TicketMasters-of-the-Universe. Well, you and I may not be consumer advocates, but we know what happens when you get more hands then necessary involved in a process. That's right, the price goes up, up, up. Suddenly, the five-dollar seat costs almost as much as the national debt.

Let's see, add $3.75 for the service charge. Service charge for what? It's more like a crime charge - a crime that they can get away with it.

Two-fifty for the handling cost. How much can it really cost to handle two one-inch by three-inch sheaths of laminated paper?

One-seventy-five for the administrative fee. With a bureaucracy like this just to get tickets, this is one charge that almost makes sense. Well, maybe not.

A $1.50 ticket surcharge. Surcharge ranks with usage fee as far as comprehensibility. The only person who understands it is the one who wrote the ordinance.

And a $1.10 state and city tax. That's better than a twenty percent tax rate on a ticket! Call your Congressman!

That five-dollar seat has just run $15.60, and that's before food, drink, and parking.

Ah yes, parking. So Mr. Politician got his 50,000 seat monument to himself, his ball team to play in the stadium, and scores of fans to fill it. Only problem (beginning to get the feeling that there are more problems with having a major league franchise in town than you realize?) is with all the covert deals cut to lure the team, there's still not enough cash generated to pay off the debt on the stadium.

So what does Mr. Politician do next? He charges $15 to park your 1974 Chevy Impala outside the stadium. For that price, it should be valet parking behind second base. Fifteen dollars is about the trade-in value of your car. Maybe you can leave the car in the lot after the game and take the bus home. That way you won't need to shell-out the towing fee when the car finally dies.

Not only does Mr. Politician institute one of the steepest parking fees this side of New York City's infamous parking structure system of "Park, Lock, Take Keys, Your Risk," he also cracks down on all illegal, pseudo-illegal, quasi-illegal, and perfectly-legal but it looks like it should be illegal on-street parking around the stadium.

To patrol this and write tickets, Mr. Politician hires forty totally unqualified people. A look at their past work experiences proves this. One person worked eight weeks at Joe's Service Station as Windshield Washer Receptacle Fluid Changer. He went through the study-at-home program pitched by Groucho Marx or some other one-time-celebrity-in-dire-need-of-info-commercial-money-if-he-were-still-alive- today.

After hiring these highly-educated individuals, Mr. Politician distributes brown polyester stretch uniforms and a summons booklet as thick as a Chicago phone book to each person. They need these stretch Bozo costumes because it's the only means to hide how physically unfit they are.

Mr. Politician then instructs them to slap one of these "Vehicle Violation Notices" on any auto that appears to be parked where it shouldn't. In effect, these Parking Nazis are granted unlimited power to issue citations. Yet, they have difficulty completing the vehicle color line on the summons. They have a hard time deciding if it's a gray or silver car.

Nevertheless, these Brownies, named for their uniform color, will write a complete book of tickets per game, or as many as possible until they can't walk any further, whichever comes first. Usually, your car is safe from the Parking Police if you've parked more than two blocks from the stadium.

But when you find a notice under the windshield wiper, be prepared to pay with your Visa card. You won't have enough cash in hand, personal checks aren't accepted, and they don't take American Express.

This isn't a cheap two-dollar expired meter violation. It's a take-out-a-second-mortgage parking fine. This is the way Mr. Politician plans to pay-off the new stadium. Aren't you glad you re-elected him?

A View from the Stands

TICKETS PLEASE

The Senators were never very good, but not much has changed in Washington. The senators they have there still aren't very good.
   Former President Nixon on his days as a Washington baseball fan

A dmission tickets are one big propaganda ploy designed by the Mind Control and Civil Obedience Office. As of this writing, this may or may not have been elevated to a Cabinet-level post in Washington. With a Democratic President, the Republicans point the finger at the White House for forming whimsical, bureaucratic positions. The Mind Control and Civil Obedience Office (or McCOO as it's known around Washington) certainly qualifies. Of course the Democrats want equal time, and they place the blame back at the Republicans. With their rebuttal, the Democratic donkeys explain McCOO was a remnant from the Reagan-Bush years of largess and conservative pork barrel politics. Soon, fingers are being shot all over the place, and not just the index finger.

   You see, McCOO was designed to control individuals' thoughts and actions. The government doesn't like when people object to laws, rules, and regulations. Now, it doesn't matter to the Feds that these mandates passed down affecting the 250 million people of this great country are designed by 535 mostly elderly white males on Capitol Hill. Doing some quick math, that means there's .0000021 of these politicians for each man, women, and child in the United States of America. This means if I wanted to call my Congressman in Washington, assuming I'd actually get

A Season with Bob the Beerman

through, I'd end up talking with his eighth hair on the second knuckle of his third finger. That is my fraction of the .0000021 of a person I'm being represented by. But the boys in D.C. still don't like when even one person dissents too vocally against the virtuous edicts emanating from Washington.

That's why McCOO was created. To get you, me, and the guy by the sea to conform. How would Washington react if even half of this nation's population marched to their own drum? Remember, these guys in D.C. thought the classic rock and roll song "Louie, Louie" was dirty and subversive.

By requiring ticketing for everything from standing in line at a deli counter, to the claim stubs for your dry cleaning, to movie admissions, the government is controlling our actions.

I say we just get rid of tickets all together. Then there would be no need for the Mr. McCOO's. Let's go to a cash basis. Five bucks hard currency gets you into the stadium. Hand the gate patrol an Abe Lincoln and then take your pick of seats. No more trying to decipher the ticket stub to locate your seat. No more dealing with ticket-checking hawks masquerading as ushers. No more scalpers charging fifty bucks for a seat with no view.

This little stub of paper is required in every corner, nook, and cranny of the ballpark, though I've never been in a cranny, and don't have any idea what one looks like. Every time you show the ticket to gain access to some part of the ball yard, the Mr. McCOO's are happy. You're conforming. And I wouldn't doubt they probably get a dime kickback every time the stub is flashed.

Let's count the times you become an obedient disciple of Mr. McCOO and present your ticket at a baseball game. Number one, entering the stadium gate. Number two, to receive the souvenir give-away immediately inside the gate. These promotional ushers want to make sure you're a paying customer before handing you the latest article of home team paraphernalia. These ushers evidently have very poor eyesight, as they could not see you enter the stadium through the turnstile five feet away from them.

Numbers three, four, and five. On the concourse, you approach three different well-groomed individuals nattily attired in color-coordinated costumes of the home team. You show each your ticket. None know where your seat is located. None work for

A View from the Stands

the home team. They are all fans from out-of-town.

Number six, you show the ticket to some guy that appears to be wearing a vending uniform. But you're not too sure he is a vendor after incidents three, four, and five. He glances at the ticket, says "that way," and motions in some direction toward the Big Dipper.

Number seven, you go to a police officer and show the stub. He can't help you, he deals only in parking tickets.

You decide to get something to eat as exhaustion begins to hit. So, number eight, you present the ticket to the concession help behind the hot dog stand. She's from a volunteer group working tonight, and it's her first time to the stadium. So you take the dog and a Coke, and show the cursed ticket to the cashier (number nine). She replies that she's not familiar with those. She can only honor the food discount tickets. You're about ready to return to your car and listen to the game on the radio.

You spot a gentleman in white shirt and navy blue tie carrying a hand-held two-way radio. This guy must be some stadium official. You show him your stub (number ten, and the McCOO's just earned a dollar) only to find out he's a stockbroker checking on the opening prices in Tokyo.

Finding a trash container to use as a dining spot, you take three deep breaths, followed by three deep sobs. You've been in the stadium for forty-five minutes, you're tired of walking, you desperately want to sit down, and your seat is still nowhere to be found. By sheer coincidence, you happen to gaze around and notice the sign for your section directly above.

Relief! You gather your belongings and proceed to the aisle's entrance. Not so fast! Just as you're about to march to your seat, you're accosted by one of the ticket-checking hawks masquerading as an usher. Where were they when you needed one? The hawk orders you to present your ticket before admittance can be granted to this section. Of course, you were so jubilant upon finding your section's entrance sign on the concourse that you're not sure what happened to your ticket.

You rifle through your pockets, you rifle through the game program, you rifle through your camera case, you're ready to rifle the usher. Finally you find the ticket in your wallet, and present it (number eleven) to the border guard, err, usher. He permits you to pass Checkpoint Charley, and in a matter of moments, you're nestled into your seat.

Knowing where your seat is, you decide to make a food-run before the first pitch. Up to the main concourse you go. While waiting in a line of indeterminable length, you decide to stock-up now so there's no need to deal with this long wait again.

A sausage sandwich with peppers and onions, an order of nachos with salsa, jalapenos, and melted cheese, a soft pretzel with globs of mustard, and two twenty-four ounce Budweiser. That should hold you over until the second inning at least.

After paying for the food and precariously balancing the load in your arms, you return to your aisle. Not so fast! The ticket-checking hawk, in her best authoritative voice, orders you to produce a ticket stub.

At least this time you know exactly where it is. In your right-front pants pocket. Only problem is with thirty-two dollars of fine ballpark delicacies in your arms leaves no free hand to remove the stub from your pocket.

So you do a balancing Wallenda act. You stack the sausage sandwich on top of the nachos, and crown it with the soft pretzel. That's in your left hand. You bite on the rim of one beer cup, taking care not chomp through the cup. The other cup is squeezed between your left forearm and beer gut. Knew the old jello-belly would come in handy for something.

But still unable to completely free a hand, you beg for clemency. Instead of offering a pardon, Helga, the ticket-checking hawk, plunges her hand into the deep reaches of your front pants pocket. This is the only time in history that a member of the opposite sex is permitted, by law, to stick their hand into your pants pocket and not be cited for indecent assault. After groping around, she pulls out the stub of a ticket.

The usher barely glances at it (number twelve) and nonchalantly remarks, "That's right, I remember you."

You're about to dump the remaining beer (whatever you haven't already spilled on yourself) from the plastic cup clinched in you jaws on this nitwit who is playing protectorate of your section. Of course the ticket-checking jerk, err, hawk, is getting a nickel split off the McCOO's dime kickback every time a ticket stub is produced.

After settling back into your seat and finishing the first course, you still have fifteen minutes until the first pitch. So you decide to empty your bladder before the dam nears the breaking point. And you remember to take the ticket and put it in the most accessible place, your shirt pocket.

At the men's room, there's a five minute wait. Not too bad, the lady's room wait is up to eighteen minutes now. When you finally get to within shouting distance of the door, you discover the reason for the delay. There is a McCOO-related person checking for ticket stubs at the entrance to the latrine (number thirteen)! You're about ready to flush him.

OK, so you survive the rest stop, though little rest came from it. Rather, your blood pressure continues to boil. You flash the ticket jerk at the top of your aisle before he could ask to see the ticket. Actually, you don't flash him, you flash the ticket stub at him (number fourteen).

In your seat once again, you devise a way to keep the ticket attached to a very visible location on your body. Scraping around underneath the seats, you're able to procure enough toxins for a special plan. A packet of sweet relish, some mustard from the soft pretzel, and a drop of Coca-Cola. Using a plastic knife, you mix the three ingredients on a discarded soda lid, while chanting a nasty curse at the ticket ushers. Once stirred to a pasty consistency, it's do the Promise margarine spread with it onto the back of your ticket. Then you slap the ticket about chest height onto your shirt. Hold it for thirty-five seconds, and, like magic, the ticket is glued to your shirt.

By using the mustard glue method to present your ticket, you're exhibiting individuality. True, you're playing to your own tune. Some may argue that you're marching to the Budweiser drum instead.

More importantly, you've got a committee of McCOO members in Washington walking forehead-first into office walls, forming think-tanks to develop some sort of legislation to control this mustard-glue and relish-rebellion.

The secret is to stay one step ahead. And if we must, we'll

move to the Lincoln-Hamilton-Jackson Standard. Greenbacks go a long way. Especially in Washington.

And then there will be no more overweight, undersexed Communist- bloc female impersonators hired as double-ticket agents by the McCOO's to harass you and stick their hands into your pants pockets.

GUYS ARE DIFFERENT THAN WOMEN

Our similarities are different.
    Dale Berra, Yogi's son

Ever notice the decor in a single male friend's apartment? In the living room, there's a couch which looks and smells like it was salvaged from an end of semester fraternity house garage sale. A folding card table with peeling veneer and two lawn chairs make the dining room set. The kitchen has a refrigerator, occupied by a twelve-pack, hot dog condiments, and a block of some green thing which could possibly be the remnants of cheese.

    It also has a sink, filled with one and one-half pots. The half-a-pot was charred down from a five-quart boiler to a pan just perfect for making Cup-of-Soup.

    Absent from the sink are dishes. That's not because they're all clean and stacked neatly in the pantry. It's because he believes in conserving water by not doing dishes. Or laundry, for that matter, but that's another story.

    His tableware consists of paper plates and the Wendy's silverware collection. Of course, had he actually owned some type of ceramic dishes and metallic knives and forks, your single male friend suddenly becomes an eligible bachelor to your single female friend.

    At certain times, these differences, even call it stereotypes, are quite apparent. Like when a guy and his female companion attend a ball game. This can or cannot be called a date, depending if you're talking to her or him.

The first thing the guy wants is a beer. They're not even to their seats, and the guy wants a beer. What type of beer? A cold beer. No lite beer here, no imports. Just a beer. What kind of beer? A Bud. No polysyllabic explanations necessary. Just a Bud.

Now, his girlfriend, what does she want? Not a Bud, of course not. How unlady-like and unsophisticated. She requests a Zima.

Next, the guy is hungry, so what does he get to fill this primeval urge. A Braaat. That's right, a bratwurst. With sauerkraut, green chili sauce, onions, relish, mustard, mayo, and ketchup. Oh, there's room for jalapenos and nacho-flavored Cheezwiz? Dump some of that on it too. No Mylanta on the side here. May as well dump extra-strength Drano down your esophagus.

His date? For her dining pleasure, she'll order a selection from the lighter fare. A tossed garden vegetable salad with fresh lemon wedges on the side, please.

Is the guy's stomach full now? Of course not. This is a baseball game, and the object is to eat as much as possible in nine innings so that you can no longer slide out of that fourteen-inch-wide seat which you fit so comfortably into before the first pitch.

So, it's desert time.

Desert time at a baseball game? Hey, this guy could be starting a whole new trend. Call Madison Avenue, call the demographers.

The guy wants peanuts for desert. The extra-salted, jumbo-sized, quadruple-shell, for elephants-only, two-pound bag.

His female acquaintance? A soft, non-dairy lite, frozen yogurt, please. What size? A small, please, in a cup if you don't mind. She doesn't need the extra calories from a sugar cone.

And what about an after dinner drink? The guy, a beer. A Bud. This is a ballpark, and the liquid refreshment has to be beer. Helps to belch up the gas from the braat anyway.

The annoying woman with whom he came? An iced cappuccino please, and a swizzle straw to sip it through.

Women are sure different than men, especially at baseball games.

A View from the Stands

BALLPARK SOUNDS

Anybody who can't tell the difference between a ball hitting wood and a ball hitting concrete must be blind.
    Yogi Berra, former Met manager.

People believe vending at a stadium would be the best job one could have, after that of ESPN's Chris Berman. You're outside in the fresh air at the ballpark, selling beer and peanuts, joking with the fans, and watching professional baseball. And you're getting paid for it, no less.

Chris Berman is stuck in the television studio. Bob the Beerman works in the great outdoors. Chris Berman gets eye strain from reading the tele-prompter. Bob the Beerman gets eye strain from watching beautiful women walk up and down the stadium aisles. Chris Berman gets to view major league baseball, but he also has to watch monster truck pulls. Bob the Beerman gets to watch major league baseball, but he also has to watch the girls in the stands.

In reality, we see very little of it. The baseball game, that is. You see, all of our work is done with our backs to the field, so our ears become our eyes. That's a slightly different twist on the term four-eyes.

And I can do a play-by-play while at work, without ever seeing a pitch, just by listening to the tones of the crowd noise, the organist at work, and the sounds of the stadium.

So let me take you through an inning of action on the field, as I worked my way up a lower level aisle between home plate and third base. The top of the inning, Lenny Dykstra at bat for the visiting Philadelphia Phillies against Bryn Smith on the mound for the Rockies. Just setting the scenario. This was all announced over the public address system. No peeking on Bob the Beerman's part.

As I emptied a beer can into a plastic cup there was the rap of the wooden bat against the baseball. "Base hit up the middle," I remarked unflinchingly, as I poured the second cold one.

Removing his wallet from a rear pocket to pay for the beer, the middle-aged man just gazed down at me in wonder. "How'd you know that? Your back was to the action. You were staring straight at those two beers you just poured."

"Karma," I answered. Actually, I can tell the sound of a ball squarely struck. It's like the sound of a wooden mallet hitting the center of a two-by-four. Hearing the crack of the bat, I knew the ball had to be hit to center field. A ball hit to the opposite field is like the mallet striking just the outer edge of the two-by-four. A baseball pulled by the batter generates an equivalent "just-off-the-center" blow of the mallet against the two-by-four. Simple high school physics. I finally learned it the third time around in that same physics class.

The crowd noise from the leadoff hit had not yet died down when a gentle buzzing crescendo rolled through, followed by a deep groan. "Dykstra ran on the first pitch. He just stole second base and moved to third. The throw got by Freddie Benavides for an error," I commented to no one in particular, as I counted out the gentleman's change.

His head shook in disbelief once again at my sightless play-by-play. "Can I take you with me on my next gambling junket?" he inquired as he handed me back a two-dollar tip. Somehow, I think, his comment was only part in jest.

The crowd was unsettled. A few moments later, a groan of dismay rifled through Mile High Stadium. "Walked the next batter on four pitches. First and third, no out," I noted aloud as I walked up the aisle.

Still uneasy, the crowd emitted a disgusted grumble after three staccato rumblings. I continued my commentary as I passed the midpoint of the aisle. "Walked the next guy on four pitches. Bases loaded for Kruk, the number four RBI guy in the league."

The poor pitching was a perfect set-up for my next line. "Buy a beer, make the Rockies' pitching look good!" That broke the tension in the crowd, and got more than a few good laughs. It also got my beer sales rolling once again. Back down to one knee, I wiped out the remaining case and a half from that one spot, the entire time keeping the crowd entertained with my adept blindside calls of the action on the field.

Thwack! Lumber against leather.

Ok, a baseball is technically cowhide, but leather creates a nice alliteration.

"Kruk just hit a rope to right-center. Cleared the bases. Pitching change time."

Sure enough, over the PA came the announcement, "The new Rockies' pitcher is . . ." A row of heads turned toward me in unison. I just gave a little wink, nodded toward the overhead speaker, and answered their unasked question. "Pitching change music."

Tink. Bat against ball, just barely. Followed by an almost sarcastic cheer. "An out. Pop-up in the infield. Daulton's out. One down."

Crack. But not solid enough. Then a more rousing round of applause. "Fly ball in play. Easy out. Two down. The Rockies may get out of this with no more damage." This was getting too easy now. And I still hadn't glanced back over my shoulder to the playing field.

A deep thud, and cheers of encouragement for the pitcher. "Struck the last guy out, and I'm out of beer. Be back soon with a fresh load right from the ice box and some more play-by-play," I exclaimed as I rolled out of sight; to the beer cooler I strolled, then back with the Lite.

The ears work fine for keeping me alert on the job, but combined with my eyes, they helped create an out-take from *Candid Camera* only an inning later.

You see, I was back in the same section where I earlier did the blind call of the game. Once again, down on one knee, back to the field, transferring a beer to the cup. The usual beerman stance. And I heard the thunk of the wood just barely striking the ball. Pop-up I thought to myself. But just as that crossed my mind, a group of fans alongside me leaped to their feet and threw their hands in the air as their gaze shifted skyward.

Uh, oh! I thought. A foul ball. And its coming this way. Take cover!

So I dropped my beer can and cup in mid-pour, covered my head, and curled into the best spontaneous fetal position possible.

This brought a giant chuckle through the surrounding crowd. Turns out they were just doing the wave. The ball was popped to the second baseman. Sometimes, one sense is better than two.

A View from the Stands

HOT AIR

On any given day ... come out to the ballpark and you'll see something different.
    Sportswriter Fred Borsch

Baseball commences each February with spring training. But no matter what baseball and television executives say, my calendar still lists it as a winter month. Those people that run the sport would like you to believe it's summer. After all, baseball is the game of summer. But doesn't the World Series end sometime near Thanksgiving?

So the fan expects to brave the elements for an early or late season game. Keep the snow gear handy for a contest in April. Break-out the football-weather clothing for the October pennant races.

But how do you prepare for some foul Fourth of July weather?

The fans would find a way, as a record crowd turned out for what was billed as "The World's Greatest, Most Spectacular Fireworks Show on Earth."

With gale-force winds more blustery than a incumbent politician battling for his constituents, the annual fireworks show appeared to be a blow out. After all, high-ranking government officials have a Constitutional obligation to protect the welfare of their citizens. So they couldn't let the show go on if it meant blazing fireworks embers landing on the ballpark's populace.

If only they were as interested in protecting the vendors in the upper decks from the havoc wreaked by the hurricane-force gusts.

You see, the freak weather created some twilight zone-type happenings in the cheap seats. With the day's highest recorded

A Season with Bob the Beerman

breezes in the metro area clocked at 91 miles per hour, one vendor timed a trash container being blown off the mezzanine-level concourse and down aisle 315 at 86 mph's.

Just ask K. Hawkeye Gross, vendor #0021. He caught the canister in the chest with the grace of a junior college defensive back meeting a NFL fullback at the goal line. His Gold Glove award-winning grab came just four rows from the second deck railing protecting those lower level suits from upper level cretins. And from airborne projectiles.

Though I was working in the next aisle, I didn't actually witness the attack on Hawkeye by the killer can. I just heard it.

Whooosh! DaDaDaDaDaDa BOOOOMM!!

The sound of the canister blown through the entrance tunnel, bouncing down the steps, and plowing into #0021. I can recognize it anywhere, anytime now. And I'm deathly afraid of it.

"What was that?" I asked a customer, diverting my attention from the beer being poured.

He replied with a deadpan face, "Oh, nothing really. Some vendor down near the railing got run over by a trash can."

Those words were just too absurd, even by my standards. And I've come up with some outlandish sayings at the ballpark.

I had to check it out. I gazed over my shoulder and down the next aisle but didn't see a thing, so I just figured this guy was getting even with me for all the B.S. that I deliver selling my wares.

So I finished pouring his six-pack of beer. Only kidding, city officials. We all know that any one individual is limited to the purchase of two brewskis at a time.

That's when I saw K. Hawkeye lifting himself off the ground, with a dazed look in his eyes and a pained sound emanating from his mouth. With no broken bones and only a slightly torn uniform, #0021 not only saved the suits in the lower level from being crushed by a jet-propelled trash container, he also held onto the wad of cash in his hand, and did not lose the vending-services-company-issued baseball cap from his head.

With each passing day, the legend of Hawkeye Gross grows larger and larger. Why, yesterday, I heard from a fan that vendor #0021 took the entire impact of a falling light tower from atop the stadium, saving the lives of tens of thousands of spectators.

A View from the Stands

THE GRAND ISLAND GANG

One of the chief duties of the fan is to engage in arguments with the man behind him. This department has been allowed to run down fearfully.
Author Robert Benchley

A s the only National League team between St. Louis and Los Angeles (well, OK, Houston is also, but who outside of Texas roots for a team in the Lone Star state? The Astros aren't exactly the Dallas Cowboys, America's team.), the Colorado Rockies have the largest geographic area from which to draw crowds. And the people have come in record numbers, from towns and cities across the globe, places with an international flavor, like Cairo, Zurich, and Moscow (Missouri, Montana, and Idaho, that is). Fans also traveled from the big cities of America like Manhattan and Cleveland, (Kansas and Wyoming) and from heritage-rich places like Dixie and Alamo, Nevada. They trekked from places unbeknown to even them, like Lost Cabin, Wyoming and Oasis, Nevada, and met people from Helper, Utah, and Winner, South Dakota at Mile High Stadium.

But the most unique group award goes to the four bus loads from Grand Island, Nebraska. I discovered rather quickly that Grand Island isn't actually an island. After all, we're talking the middle of the United States, the Great Plains. The nearest body of water was the floodwaters from the Mississippi River. With this geography lesson in mind, any people who name their town an island have to be "special."

Out-of-town fans make it an event when they travel to a ball game. The Grand Island Gang made it a three-day party. They came to Denver for a late July weekend series with St. Louis, and had so much fun that one bus load stayed for the Monday game against the Atlanta Braves. They never left their seats in sections 413 and 414, probably not even to relieve themselves. Partially protected from the elements by the top deck's overhang, they were there when I punched out at night and when I returned for the next day's game.

And during the games, if I was anywhere in the stadium, I had to be there. With them. With beer. With peanuts. With CrackerJack. With red ropes. That's licorice for the uninformed. Ever try to bellow "LICORICE!" while carry a case of beer and a load of 'nuts and ropes? It has a mashed potato sound quality, kind of like "LCCRRRCSCH."

If I tried to serve another aisle, I was quickly reprimanded with Grand Island chants of "BRING BACK BOB! BEAT BOB'S BUTT!" Restocking my beer load was the only way to escape the insanity. The Grand Island Gang gave me three and a half minutes to sprint back to my commissary and refill. Or in this case, reload, as I needed a full arsenal of artillery. And not just food products. Verbal weaponry was key to sparring with these folks.

When I failed to beat the time limit, they came down hard. "BOB'S A SLACKER!" they jeered.

So I blamed it on the hot dog man. "The wiener man couldn't figure how to change five one dollar bills into a five-spot," I explained. "He slowed down the entire vending operation. Stadium-wide."

This usually won back the Grand Island Gang. And if it didn't, I always made sure to pour some water over my head to make it appear I had been sweating profusely as I did the broken field run back to their section lugging at least ten pounds of peanuts, thirty red ropes, and two cases of ice-covered beer. You'd be surprised how many sales you can get with the old sweat-appeal.

And did they ever love the sweat dripping, beer-pouring work ethic routine. By the third inning, they were mesmerized with my power-pour and peanut-pitch double play. By then, the more musically inclined of the Grand Island Gang started synchronizing the chants directed at me with the music carried over the public

23

address system. When the *Adams Family* theme song was played, each interlude was greeted with a staccato chorus of "BOB'S BEER!" instead of the more traditional snapping of the fingers a la Gomez, Morticia, Lurch, and Uncle Fester.

When the Beach Boys' "California Girls" was piped over the speakers, an energetic group of Grand Island girls stood and did their own rendition. Suddenly, it was "I wish we all could be the Bobster's girls" replacing "I wish they all could be California girls." I was flattered. Unfortunately, I became so caught up in the passion of the moment (figuratively, not literally), I forgot to get any phone numbers. It would have been long distance any way.

During a between inning break, another one of the Grand Island chorus girls performed a solo rendition to the Beatles' "Help." Gyrating to the music with the rock and roll theatrics of John, Paul, George, and Ringo, this Grand Island girl captivated the surrounding crowd. It was karaoke at its finest. As she closed out the song with "Won't you please help me? help me help me oooh," the fans in the second level erupted with wild applause. Even the home plate umpire held up the first pitch of the inning to check over his shoulder and see what caused the commotion.

The St. Louis series set a major league attendance mark for a four-game series, and in the annals of the Rockies' first season, the Grand Island Gang left its mark as the most boisterous group.

FAMILY SECTION

Baseball, my son, is the cornerstone of civilization.
   Dagwood Bumstead, as drawn by Chic Young

S tadiums and arenas throughout the country now provide alternative seating arrangements to the time-honored ballpark tradition of wedging as many broad-butts into as few splintered, narrow seats as possible. It's called the "Comfortable Seating Section." Couches, love seats, and recliners have replaced the cracked-plastic-with-spilled-Coca-Cola-stained seats.

Ok, it's a fib. There is no such thing as a comfortable stadium seat, let alone a "Comfortable Seating Section."

But there are "Family" and "No Alcohol" sections. In concept, there is a certain rationality to attempts by local municipalities, in conjunction with professional sports teams, to offer the most hospitable atmosphere in which to watch a game. Gee, that sounds like a politician speaking - long-winded and difficult to understand.

But after all, who wants some sauced fan spilling beer on your new $225 North Face ski jacket? Ski jacket?!? Hey, in any town outside of Los Angeles, it's perfectly appropriate outerwear for an early season game.

Who wants your children exposed to foul-mouthed cretins? Who wants to sit down-wind from a chain-smoking, foul-odored transient?

At one time or another, anyone who has ever attended more than one professional sporting event has had to cope with Pigpen on the right and Norman Bates on the left. It's not like this has never happened before. But, if a section is provided to free oneself from those pseudo-human types with undesirable traits and habits, why not take advantage? It would be like locking yourself in a safe house with the riff-raff outside. Nothing like a little isolationism, eh?

Of course, the possibilities are endless for various "theme" sections that could be designated at the stadium. How about a "Baseball Instructional Section," where all those who have no clue about the American pastime can sit?

Most of these will be foreigners who know only the complete rules of soccer and cricket. To them, baseball is too boring. Give me a break, when's the last time you saw an eight to seven soccer score? So these guests to our country never developed an interest in our national devotion. But they do understand certain subtleties of our game such as cold beer and hot dogs and women in skimpy tops at the ballpark.

The other group most likely to be represented in the "Baseball Instructional Section" would be women whose husbands' athletic activities are limited to channel surfing and sidewalk sweeping. These husbands never play sports. Fly fishing is too taxing. The only team these guys made in high school was the chess team, and they got winded playing it. Therefore, their spouses were never exposed to sports either. After living with a lack of football, baseball, and golf on television, these women decided to take the initiative and learn something about sports. What better way than in the "Baseball Instructional Section"?

There, they will be educated to the rules and history of the game by a retired career sub-.200 hitting back-up infielder who may or may not speak fluent English. Hundreds of ex-jocks could be recruited to lead this group. After all, there are only so many TV commentator spots available to guys that can no longer hit the curve ball.

Another theme section could be the "No Smoking Section." This could be an instructional area also. Why not hire a cardiologist to extoll the virtues of a smokeless environment and provide directions on how to use the nicotine patch for those kicking the habit?

A sister section to this could be the "Cigar Smoking Only

Section." No one, except those smoking the Fidel Castro Cuban Special autographed models, appreciates sitting next to a person puffing away on industrial strength cancer sticks. The fumes are more noxious than those in a construction site Port-O-Let. Banish these refugees. Give them their own section, somewhere removed from all other life forms, somewhere over the rainbow. Or maybe in Cuba.

So as not to discriminate, a "Pipe Smoking Only Section" would be required. Nowadays, only great grandfathers, affluent aristocrats, and the very sophisticated (snobs) smoke pipes. This section would be very small. Everyone here could comfortably be seated in a Port-O-Let.

And don't forget the "Teenage Boys with Guns Section." The government has attempted to rectify this gang problem of the 1990's through numerous band-aid programs. Why not offer free admission to all boys entering with a gun. Herd them into the cheap seats, the Rockpile. Then once it's filled with youths named Viper, Assassin, and PitBull, raise the super-secret high voltage fence around the section, and sentence them to hard labor on the rock pile.

Isn't it a bit peculiar that ushers check for beer and liquor smuggled illegally into the stadium but not guns or knives? And how is it that vendors can't serve beer in its aluminum can to the fans, but must rather pour the beer into a plastic cup? It's a safety issue, officials say, for fear of the can being thrown onto the field. Yet deadly weapons can be brought into the ballpark. Don't you feel safe and secure now?

One section that already exists is the "Family Section." There's no drinking, smoking, or cursing allowed. That's fine, I guess. Unless you happen to get tickets for that section from a friend but don't realize you're neighbors with Ward, June, Wally, and the Beaver Cleaver.

Ignorant to the seat location, you invite three of your most obnoxious, unruly, buddies who like to eat, drink, and be merry in as many crude ways as possible. You arrive at the seats carrying a small bar's worth of beer in your hands and a leggy blond usherette on your shoulders. Only when sitting down are you advised by the usherette that the tickets are for the "Family Section" and that everything you've bought and done in the last fifteen minutes is not permitted there. You and your friends immediately take a vow not to invite to the next Super Bowl party the friend who gave you the tickets without a "Family Section" location disclaimer.

Then there is the problem defining family. Ward, June, Wally and Beaver Cleaver obviously qualify. But does Murphy Brown and her baby? What about other single mothers with children who don't have the celebrity status of Murph? And what about other non-traditional families?

The best solution may be a "No-Vice Section." This would cover the alcohol, tobacco, firearms, and family values issues under one umbrella. But then, who would have any fun at a ball game?

REMEMBER ME - I SAW YOU OPENING DAY

We've seen history made here today, a performance which probably never will be duplicated.
   Attributed to ex-home run king Babe Ruth

B y the end of the Colorado Rockies' first season, four million-plus fans will have passed through Mile High Stadium's turnstiles. And half of them will profess to attending the first game of the inaugural year against the Montreal Expos. And roughly half of them will swear that they met Bob the Beerman on that memorable Friday afternoon in April. So that means I met approximately one million Rockies' zealots in a span of about five hours. And they all remembered my name. Was I supposed to recall each of theirs? I try.

Now some names are easier than the others. Bob is a good guess to start when I probe the recesses of my mind in search of fans' names. Especially after not seeing them for a couple of months.

You see, all the other Bobs in the world, or at least at the ballpark, seem to identify with the celebrity status of Bob the Beerman No longer are they Just Bob. They share the same first name with Bob the Beerman, Hollywood Bob, America's Beerman.

They are proud to extend their hand and exude that their name is also Bob. So when some fan asks if I remember them from the million people I met opening day, I reply with, "Could it be Bob?"

If right, I look like a genius. The fan thanks me for remembering his name, and buys my case of beer. With a big tip on the side. If wrong, the fan tells me his name is Wyatt. Or Walter, William, or Wynn, and on opening day he sat down the right field line in section 103, and bought four beers from me.

Then I act as if I'm searching my memory banks. After a deliberate pause, I'll nod my head and confirm to him that I do, in fact, remember him from the one million fans I met during the first game. Then I ask if he also needs four beers this time. So flattered that Bob the Beerman remembers him, he orders six beers.

Over the duration of the season, so many different fans have come to me, asking if I remember them from the first meeting on opening day. Each person was sitting in a different location. Some sat upstairs along the third base line. Others were down behind the visiting team's dugout. Some were in the south stands. And others were in Brooklyn's. All swear they met me that day, and that I poured them a couple of cold ones.

I suppose it's possible I met them all. More than once, fans have called me omnipresent. Yet, I know I couldn't have been vending both upstairs and downstairs at the same time. And besides, it's a no-no under ARA policies.

So many people, located in different sections across the stadium on opening day, claimed to have met me. I'm not even certain what level and sections I worked. I do know it couldn't have been the east stands, because I was nowhere near Eric Young's leadoff home run to left field. Yet a million fans swore that I poured them a beer there. And the same million swore Young's history-making home run just glanced off their outstretched hands.

A Season with Bob the Beerman

BALLPARK ECONOMICS

A nickel ain't worth a dime anymore.
    Yogi Berra, Yankee Hall of Fame catcher

When journeying to the stadium for a ball game, to root on the home team and scope the opposite sex, fans know to bring a hefty wad of cash, or at least a second mortgage. Let's face it, nothing's cheap at the ballpark. Even the players charge for autographs. Of course, the worse the team (or player), the less they charge. Allegedly, there's been a handful of players who have been known to pay signature seekers to seek their signatures.

For the average beer drinker, err, fan, the sum demanded for a stars' signature equals a half-year's after tax income. Rather than spend junior's college education fund to buy a star's John Hancock, most fans grudgingly part with their dollars on the ballpark's fine dining and shopping opportunities.

Of course, you'd be surprised (well, probably not) how many disbelieving looks us vendors get when we say it's three bucks for an eight-ounce package of styrofoam, err, stale, err salted peanuts, two seventy-five for a twelve-ounce beer, and two-fifty for a jumbo hot dog That's a fatter version of the traditional dirty water (boiled) hot dog on a soggy bun. No, that's not sesame seeds on the hot dog roll, it's Grandpa Munster's next batch of penicillin fermenting to mold.

Hey, this is a ballpark and nothing is cheap. Want an inexpensive stadium meal? Do the blue light special thing at the K-Mart cafeteria before the game. It makes the stadium food seem as if it was prepared by Chef Claude of the Culinary Institute, and at a

A View from the Stands

bargain basement value.

But peanuts at three dollars a pop? Isn't that outrageous?

Not when you consider Jimmy Carter has been out of the White House for over a dozen years and needs money to live. How much do you think he makes building thatched houses in third world nations? That's why the peanuts are so expensive. The economy is so tough even ex-Presidents need a second income.

At least kids are indiscriminate consumers. They're wiser to ballpark economics than most realize. Kids know when daddy's buying. And most have developed an attack plan to guarantee the old man's wallet will be much thinner on the trip home after the game.

Junior's game plan usually goes something like this. Entering the stadium, he gets the program with scorecard for three dollars and drops a hint how great the autographed baseball and pennant look. It's a classic set-up for the late game buying frenzy.

Trying to find your seats, Junior points out every food stand along the way.

"Look, a Taco Bell, a Subway sandwich place, and Domino's. Do you think they'll deliver to our seats?"

Of course, Dad starts feeling guilty. So, at the next concession stand, he asks what Junior would like to eat.

Well, this is the 1990's, and the ballpark food fare reads like a menu at a yuppie restaurant. Forget the hot dog and soda. Junior wants a turkey and melted Brie sandwich on whole wheat with grey poupon and a pasta vinaigrette salad on the side. Well, actually, white bread. No one under the age of sixteen has any concept of the varieties of bread other than sliced white Wonder-Bread.

It's a good thing Evian isn't sold in the stadium, or Junior would be chugging it to wash down his meal. Dad settles for a dog and hopes to find a beerman peddling a Coors Light.

Finding their seats, Junior devours his traditional stadium food in nanoseconds. Let's see - nine dollars of food consumed in a tad over three minutes. Doing some quick math, Dad concludes it costs $180 an hour to feed Junior. Instantly, the light bulb goes on in Dad's brain. Get Junior a job as a taste tester for some food company and they'd be able to afford something better than the

A Season with Bob the Beerman

Bob Uecker seats they're occupying.

Soon they realize there is no way to sneak by the hospitality ushers (the stadium ticket-checking Gestapo) to upgrade into better seats. Not even a ten-spot would do the trick. If this were Yankee Stadium in New York, they would now be sitting comfortably four rows behind the visiting team's dugout.

Junior plans the next salvo.

"Since we're sitting in the cheap seats, do you think I can get a Starter warm-up jacket?" Junior asks.

Big request, big money, but Junior, expecting Dad to say no, uses it as a bargaining ploy. This comes in handy in the eighth inning. That's when Junior hits Dad for the baseball cap, official team sweat shirt, and autographed ball.

But now it's early in the game, and the hot dog vendor comes strolling by with peanuts in the side bag and red ropes around his neck. Junior quickly orders one of each, covering both the salt and sugar food groups, and devours the dog before Dad asks "Do you really need this food?"

Between chomps on the licorice, Junior replies, "I changed my mind on the warm-up. Besides, I'm a growing boy, and I need my nutrients."

Junior's enterprising abilities to strike a favorable deal with Dad for his favorite team's paraphernalia is growing as fast as his appetite.

As the game settles into a mid-inning lull, so does Junior with his appetite. Well, maybe Junior is just curbing his hunger for food and preparing to unleash a hunger for souvenirs.

And what perfect timing, as the memorabilia man meanders down the aisle, hustling his wares.

"Look at all the stuff!" Junior exclaims. Pennants, baseballs, caps, and mitts; a plethora of soon to be boxed basement paraphernalia.

Junior lets this fellow pass without asking dad to buy him anything. He just stares with sad puppy dog eyes. As Dad looks away with guilt, Junior discretely gives the vendor hand signals to return in the seventh inning. The set-up for the kill begins.

As the top of the sixth inning arrives, Junior tells Dad he has to do number two. So the two hike the steps to the rest room.

A View from the Stands

Now Junior doesn't really need a potty stop. He knows there is a great souvenir booth just past the bathroom. So Junior goes through the motions in the men's room, giving Dad a few minutes alone outside. Strategic planning here. Dad peruses the souvenir stand while waiting.

Allowing Dad enough time to check-out all the items, Junior emerges from the bathroom. "Could I have the gray Champion sweat shirt with the team name on it? Pleeease, Dad?" Junior asks, noticing Dad's focus.

Still remorseful from the sad eyes syndrome, Dad forks over thirty-five bucks for a children's medium size. Of course, there's about only a dollar seventy-five worth of material used in the shirt. Enough fabric to barely cover a small pillow.

No sooner do they arrive back to the seats than the hawker reappears. Knowing how this game is played from his numerous years selling at stadiums, the ball park Stuffman plays to Dad.

"What was it that you wanted, sir," the Stuffman inquires innocently.

Dad wears a perplexed look. The Stuffman wears a look of an imminent sale. Junior wears his gray Champion sweat shirt.

Junior doesn't miss a beat. Before Dad could tell the Stuffman that he has the wrong person, Junior chimes in, "A pennant and autographed baseball, please."

Dad's dumbfounded. Before Dad's lips could move, the Stuffman gives the merchandise to Junior with one hand, and his other hand is outstretched awaiting payment. Out of reflex action developed while shopping with his wife, Dad reaches into a back pocket, yanks out his wallet, and shells over another thirty-one bucks. Shell-shocked describes Dad.

Is the financial pillage complete? Nope.

Leaving the stadium, Junior stops at the last concession stand before the exit gates. Taking a yearbook into his hands, he tells Dad, "It'll be a much quieter ride home if I had this book to look at." Seven dollars and fifty cents later, they are on the way to remote parking lot ZZ.

Just maybe, Junior's college costs will be less than a day at the ball game.

A Season with Bob the Beerman

THE OPPOSITE SEX

A great catch is like watching girls go by - the last one you see is always the prettiest.
        Bob Gibson, flame-throwing St. Louis Cardinal Hall of Famer

As vendors, we're supposed to put the fan first; give service with a smile. And I whole heartily agree with that. I believe in giving whatever is necessary to make the stay at the stadium as enjoyable as possible. Unfortunately (or perhaps fortunately), not only do some of the female fans take this quite literally, but they also continue it outside of the park fences.

Like the time I reached my parked car after the game to find a freshly cut red rose on the windshield. Attached was a short poem, written in what appeared to be lipstick - though I never did get the lab reports back on it, and an invitation to dinner with a phone number. But I passed on this one because I recognized the suggested restaurant as merely a two-star joint.

Besides, I'm a firm believer in the adage "a picture is worth a thousand words," and with no picture, I'm not going to waste my words. I'll be needing those words in the written form for this book.

Then there was the woman who slyly abandoned her date in section 428 and blocked my path as I entered the concourse under the stands. She cornered me against a closed cotton candy concession booth, and would not allow me back into the seating area to hawk my goods until she got my name (it really is Bob) and accepted an offer for a post- game drink at Brooklyn's Bar & Grill.

35

A View from the Stands

I had noticed her an inning earlier as I hiked up an aisle and sold her and her companion a couple of beers. Her features were as striking as his were imposing. So, before I committed to her invite, I made sure that the big baggage on her arm wouldn't be there.

"Guaranteed," she replied, and sealed it with a kiss on the cheek.

Good thing it wasn't a toasting hot day, or she would have received a mouthful of body salt that more typically forms on my face while working.

Ah, yes, Brooklyn's. Strange things have happened to me there in the post-game. A woman recognized me at the bar, even though I was out of costume, err, uniform. She started buying rounds for both of us. After the third one, she excused herself. Nature had called for a visit to the ladies' room. No sooner did she turn the corner into the rest room hallway than did another women sidle up to me at the bar and buy a round. Nature works in funny ways.

If I didn't know better, I would have sworn that the second women was monitoring the first's drink consumption. It seemed as if the second female was waiting for the instant when the first's bladder burst to occupy the vacated spot next to me.

At the stadium, it's always helpful when some of the more mature vendors (i.e., married ones) are on the look-out for eligible members of the opposite sex.

No, not for themselves. For those of us without significant others.

It's a no brainer. The married hawkers do the prescreening. Then they inform the lucky vendor of the section, row, and seat number along with a scouting report on the prospect. People of the opposite sex are rated on a four-level scale: 1. Check this one out. 2. Have I got one for you. 3. Wine 'em and dine 'em. 4. Wants to know if you're available.

The key to understanding the guidelines are simple.

A one - go by the seat, look, and ogle discretely. Usually mirrored Ray Ban sunglass help. Drool a little, but don't slobber, it makes a mess of your uniform. Then pour a beer for a person two rows in front of the prospective victim so you can prolong the gaze. Then keep moving. But make sure to pass by every inning.

A two - go by the seat, look, smile warmly, then let the old charm take over. From there, it's wherever fate lands.

A three does not need fate. It's go by the seat, look, ask what the person does for a living, and set a dinner date for the first Friday evening there's no scheduled home game. Never suggest to a three to meet her at Brooklyn's after the game.

A four - it's go by the seat, look, and ask if she prefers home or away games.

Yes, this sexist game, if you will, does exist at the stadium.

A pair of single female vendors told me they've had some great successes with the ratings network.

A View from the Stands

AWAY GAMES

If the people don't want to come out to the park, nobody's going to stop them.
  Yogi Berra, former Yankee manager

Unfortunately for die-hard local fans, major league baseball requires your hometown team to play half its games on the road. For baseball widows and widowers, this is the only time the lawn is mowed, the hedges trimmed, the gutters cleaned, and the sloth removed from the living room Lazy-Boy. And for the players, it's an opportunity to sample seafood from San Francisco, knishes from New York, and cheesesteaks from Philadelphia. Also, it's the time to escape the crush of the fans' swell and the swirl of the hometown media.

I know that feeling well. When the team is out of town, Bob the Beerman does likewise. So maybe I didn't make it to Wrigley or Riverfront, Fenway, Camden Yards, or Yankee Stadium. I went to the left coast instead. No need to be a brain surgeon on this one. Where would you rather be people watching, the South Bronx or Malibu??

While in California, I had five big-league parks from which to choose. And it took about as long to make a decision as to which stadium to see a game as it takes a New Yorker to boo the Mets.

So, it had to be Candlestick Park, right? The place shaken by the quake in the 1989 World Series by the Bay. Home of both the team with one of the best records and the player with the most talent. The San Francisco Giants and Barry Bonds, that is.

Nah, I passed. As Mark Twain said (or maybe didn't say,

A Season with Bob the Beerman

depending on your sources. And half of my sources just returned from a liquid lunch), "The coldest winter I ever spent was a summer in San Francisco." Now why on earth would I want to face winter in the middle of August?

Then it had to be the team across the Bay? Let's be serious. Who plays for the A's anymore? Jose Canseco? Gone. Rickey Henderson? Gone. The fans? Gone.

Would you pay to see these guys play? Not many people in Oakland do. Perhaps the A's offices at Oakland-Alameda County Stadium need an earth-moving-sized shake-up. It would add some character to a perfectly nondescript stadium and what's become an equally nondescript organization. Even the ballpark's name is bad. Goes with the team.

Ok, then how about farther south into Orange County, Disneyland, and the Big A, the home of the California Angels. With a ballpark named the Big A (actually Anaheim Stadium, but people have been calling it the Big A for years), would you want to see a game there? The only memorable thing about this park was a giant, free-standing "A" encircled with an angel's halo (no joke) in the parking area beyond center field. Only in the land of Mickey and Minnie.

Then onto Jack Murphy Stadium in San Diego. The Padres' owners conducted a fire sale of their best players in an effort to reduce the payroll. So why go see a talentless team in an impressionless stadium?

The choice, of course, Dodger Stadium, the only place to view baseball in California. If I'm going to do it, I'm going to do it right. A palace of a park, set among the palm trees on a plateau overlooking downtown Los Angeles. If the cookie-cutter stadiums are antiseptic, then Dodger Stadium is quintessential Tinseltown. Easy access, wide seats, great sight lines (in more ways than one), real grass. And Hollywood celebrities galore - when the team is good.

Somehow, you get the sense that when old ballplayers die, they want to go to Dodger Stadium, not to heaven.

And when Bob the Beerman goes to Dodger Stadium, he wants good seats. The laid-back hospitality of Southern California took care of this. You see, the ticket booth attendant, a perfect image of Dodger manager Tommy Lasorda's brother, gave us the skinny on good seats.

"Monday night game, they're not playing good ball, Colorado Rockies in town, there will be a lot of no-shows. Buy the tickets along the foul line, work your way down, and jump into some empties you see behind the dugouts. Best way to get close to the action."

Only in LA. In New York, it would have cost a twenty to a sweaty-palmed usher for a comparable spot.

The advice worked perfectly. As game time neared, we worked our way to field level and found three empty seats twelve rows behind the first base dugout. Good thing a bad draw like the Rockies were in town. If the Giants were invading LA, we may have been stuck sitting in the ticketed seat.

And isn't it ironic that Bob the Beerman chooses to catch a game in Los Angeles, and who is in town but Colorado? First Rockies' game I actually got to see in its entirety and while drinking beer, not pouring them.

Unfortunately, there were no Bob the Beermen in Dodger Stadium selling suds in the stands. Or Bill or Bud the Beerman either. Brews were sold only on the concourse. So it was climb eight rows and a quick seven paces across the concourse to the beer bar.

There's something about being served a cold one in your seat at the ballpark without missing a pitch. I'd pay a premium for the service. After all, do you think the guy that invented the remote control liked to get out of his seat to turn TV channels??

Sitting on the aisle, I was the chosen one to handle beer procurement. So off I went, knowing very well that I could be missing a grand slam or a triple play. Ok, ok, that's a gross exaggeration. From the first concourse just rows behind our seats, the entire playing field was in view.

The next dilemma encountered was that one individual was permitted to purchase only two twelve-ounce beers for $3.75 each, but there were three of us. And you thought my prices were expensive??

So it was time to turn on the Bob the Beerman charm. I started schmoozing with the beer bar attendant, telling him that

A Season with Bob the Beerman

I'm with the Rockies.

Well, I am. I'm a beerman for them.

It turns out that this exact same concessionaire had the entourage of Rockies' owner Jerry McMorris doing the beer-run thing to his bar during the last trip the Rockies made to LA. When Nelson (not his real name. We don't want him to lose his job.) heard my line about being with the Rockies, he quickly replied, "For you Mr. McMorris, three coming right up."

Hey, Jerry, thanks for laying the groundwork for me on your first visit to Dodger Stadium.

Vending in the stands was low-key and uninspired by the Dodger hawkers. Not to mention beer-less, and with little food variety. None had the charisma of good old Nelson (not his real name). Peanuts were sold, but in small three and three-quarter ounce bags for $1.75. Please make note they're still more expensive than the eight-ounce bag I sell. And for all the fanfare the Dodger vendors receive for pitching peanuts to the purchaser, it's not a difficult feat when the aisles are only twenty rows long and each row has just eight to twelve seats. Compare that to the forty-something rows and twenty-five seats per row on average where I pitch peanuts. Even my kid sister could toss those whimpy Dodger peanut bags clear across the section.

Then there were the Cool-a-Coos hawkers. For the uneducated, and I admit to being one, a Kool-a-Koos is an ice cream type sandwich with vanilla, chocolate, and chocolate chips mixed together in some way, shape, fashion, or form. Only some elf knows the exact ingredients and procedure. The vendors had no clue to the composition. Also, please note the two spelling alternatives above. When asked to spell what they were selling, once again the vendors had no clue. Talk about air.

And the answer to a burning question all are anxiously awaiting, no they don't sell sushi at Dodger Stadium. This is according to Nelson (still not his real name). After all, we all know and trust Nelson. And just call me Bob McMorris.

A View from the Stands

CELEBRITY ROW

You can plant two thousand rows of corn with the fertilizer Lasorda spreads around.
  Sportscaster and former catcher Joe Garagiola on Dodger manager Tommy Lasorda

While it may not have the same publicity impact as being photographed leaving Planet Hollywood, Madonna's apartment, or the Kennedy Compound, being seen at a baseball game can give the rich and famous person's career enough of a boost to sell a few extra tickets to his latest movie. Of course, if the film was any good, he wouldn't have to make an appearance at a ball game to do promotional work. But it still beats guesting on *The Geraldo Show*.

The list of who's who at the ballpark's celebrity row ranges from expected, to surprising, to why aren't they here.

Woody and Mia were no-shows, but that's no surprise.

Neither of the Michael J's were ever spotted, but that's no surprise either when considering how elusive both Mr. Jackson and Mr. Jordan were this past year.

And speaking of Jacks, Nicholson didn't make any appearances outside of games in Los Angeles, New York, and Chicago.

Two mouths that roared didn't do any roaring in my sections. Never did see Howard Stern or Rush Limbaugh around the stadium. All the hot dog vendors could attest to it also. None sold relish and mustard to anyone resembling Howard, and no one had any Limbaugh look-alike order a dozen hot dogs from them.

So which celebs made it to town??

Lyle Lovett was here one day, and the entire vending crew

A Season with Bob the Beerman

was searching for his spouse Julia Roberts. You see, Lovett gave a concert across the street at the sports arena at the same time as the baseball game. Bunch of us beermen were going to bolt early and try to pull double duty at the concert in hopes of finding Ms. Roberts. Sorry to report, none of us spotted her.

Lyle and Julia were a one-shot long shot, but every Sunday afternoon brought former Presidential hopeful Gary Hart to the stadium. And every Sunday he had illicit peanuts with him. These weren't the ballpark variety. These were those contraband ones bought outside the gates and snuck in. But let's be grateful it was just nuts and not arms for hostages being smuggled.

For a politician, Hart had an uncanny sense of humor. One sizzling-hot midsummer game, I was working his aisle like a construction worker at a thrice delayed opening of a new international airport. Actually, I was working much harder than that.

Beer was being passed down row fourteen, peanuts to row eleven, CrackerJack to row ten, money coming back from rows fifteen, fourteen, and ten. When all the transactions were complete, I had come up short four dollars. So I waved to the people who were slow to the wallet and yelled, "I'm short. I need more money. I'm having a funding problem."

Without missing a beat, Hart jumped in, "I'm familiar with that. I had the same problem a few years back."

Somehow, I'd rather have the funding problem running for president than running for beer.

Every Friday night game brought former NBA great and Denver Nuggets' coach Dan Issel to the ballpark. A member of the Basketball Hall of Fame, the Horse thus qualifies for celebrity status. Though with a nickname like the Horse, that's kind of shaky.

The Duke was a rough and tumble nickname for John Wayne, who never made it to the ballpark. Magic could only be the Los Angeles Lakers' great Earvin "Magic" Johnson, and I didn't see him at any games either. Tricky Dick evokes memories of embattled Watergate President Richard Nixon, who wasn't at any games. But the Horse? Who coined that nickname?

Now, we all know that Dan wasn't baptized Horse. Had to be some Oscar Madison sportswriter that penned the name. Heck, even the Lone Ranger's horse was called Silver, not just Horse.

Another celeb from the sports community who would make special guest appearances in his season VIP Field Box seats was John Elway. The Broncos' All-Pro quarterback showed opening day. For the balance of the season, those seats were usually occupied by individuals that strangely did not resemble John in the least bit.

But us vendors had a great time with Elway's seats. Whenever we approached his seats, we would always yell, "Two beers coming right up, Mr. Elway!" That always got the fans attention, and inevitably, they would stop us to ask where John was sitting. At that point, we would hit them with a beer sales pitch. Could always count on unloading half a case of beer around Elway's section with this routine.

Reportedly seen in or near celebrity row were government figureheads. Now, I say reportedly, because it was never confirmed, but Vice-President Dan Quayle allegedly took in a game while in the city on business for President Clinton. Unfortunately, the Prez didn't make it to any games. Something about no McDonald's in the stadium.

Ooops, I blundered. I just made Dan Quayle a famous person. Sorry about that Dan, didn't mean to grant you that notoriety. We all know you're not Vice-President anymore. Bill Clinton's second in command is, a, err, umm, give me a second here. Oh, now I remember, the guy who one night co-hosted *The Late Show with David Letterman*. Call him Al, Gore.

Anyway, this guy supposedly showed with an entourage of secret service personnel to see an early season game, but no one could (or would - smells of a cover-up to me) confirm that Vice-President what's-his-name was actually at the park.

Two rich and famous individuals who I'll be happy to confirm appeared at a game I worked were Ted Turner and Jane Fonda. Now, Ted and Jane jetted in from their ranch in Montana to watch the team they own, the Atlanta Braves.

They arrived in a white stretch limousine in the second inning. As the car door flew open and Ted and Jane emerged, the fans on the concourse parted like the Red Sea before Charlton Heston. Nope, Charlie didn't attend any games I worked.

A Season with Bob the Beerman

Escorted to VIP seats in the first row directly behind the home plate screen, the former *Time* magazine Man of the Year and his movie star wife had the crowd abuzz.

Now, before the game, us vendors were joking about Ted and Jane making an appearance. After all, it was the Braves' first appearance in town, and there was hope that the dynamic duo (not Batman and Robin - didn't see them at any games either) would show.

Well, I didn't know they were in the stadium until one of the most attractive hospitality usherettes grabbed me as I walked across the lower concourse after refilling with cold beer.

Leading me toward the aisle, she remarked, "Bob, I need a beerman with a fresh case from the cooler. For some VIP's down front."

Well, I met all the requirements there. "Who is it?" I asked.

"Ted Turner and Jane Fonda, but be low key about it. Don't ask them for their autographs."

"Ask them for their autographs? I'm Bob the Beerman, Beercan Bob, The Bobster, America's Beerman. I'm more used to giving them out then asking for them."

No sooner had these words left my mouth then a youngster sitting on the end of a row tapped me on the arm as I passed and asked if I could sign his program. Total disbelief painted the usherette's face. I paused only briefly enough to pen my signature and told the youth that I'd be back in a few minutes to talk with him after pouring a couple of beers for some famous people down front.

Reaching Ted and Jane's seat, I knelt to one knee. Not in reverence, that's just my standard beer pouring stance.

"Two beers, please," Ted ordered in a very business-like, matter-of-fact tone, without changing his gaze from the field.

As I cracked the first cold one, I noticed about ten full cups of beer under their seats. "What's wrong with these beers down here?" I asked.

Switching his view from the field, Ted answered. "Those beers were bought for us by the fans. It's the wrong brand. We don't drink that crap."

I chuckled. Guess no matter who you are or where you are,

A View from the Stands

every fan has a beer preference. So I poured two of my alternative brand beers, handed them to Ted and Jane, and collected the money. He gave me a hundred dollar bill and told me to keep the change - just kidding. Then I was on my way back up the aisle to see the youngster whose scorecard I had just autographed.

For those with inquiring minds, want to know what beer Ted and Jane preferred and which one they dissed?? Well, Coors Light, Budweiser, and Miller Genuine Draft were the three beers vended in the stands at that time. And the one brand that Ted and Jane let ferment under their seats was . . .

Sorry, I can't divulge this bit of information.

You see, Coors has a big stake in the team, Budweiser is underwriting this book (I wish), and I'm best friends with the Miller account representative. Looks like I'm forced to carry this secret to my grave.

Also for those with inquiring minds, yes Jane did fall asleep on Ted's shoulder, just as she had on national television during the last two World Series in which the Braves played.

Perhaps one person conspicuous by his absence from the ballpark was the Mayor. None of the vendors saw him in the stands, and at last count there was 587 of us during the course of the season. I personally wanted to sell him a beer. And make him show me his ID. After all, it's the Mayor's law that requires the vendors to proof everyone purchasing a beer that appears to be under the age of forty. And you and I both thought the drinking age was twenty-one. Could embarrassment with this rule be the reason the Mayor stayed away from the stands?

Heck, even the Pope made it to the stadium this year.

A Season with Bob the Beerman

I Want You To Buy That Person A Beer

Van Mungo liked to drink a bit. Anything. Even hair tonic.
   Leo Durocher, former Chicago Cub manager

A bar is the number one place to meet a member of the opposite sex, but you would be surprised how much of that type hunting occurs at a baseball game. Bartenders like ex-pitcher Sam Malone have the inside scoop on the singles action. But at the ballpark, Bob the Beerman is as close as you get to a bartender. I may not be able to poor a stiff one, at least not here at the ballpark, but I hear some of the best lines. I know who's buying whom a drink, and see who's making all the moves.

Occasionally, I get paid by a fan's co-worker to make the moves, or at least embarrass someone until the person turns the color of a Phillies' baseball cap. It's nothing too severe. Like requiring some 50 year-old to present his ID for a bag of peanuts, or asking if the straw Panama hat is functional - like protecting the bald spot from the sun.

Sometimes, the co-workers are ruthless, mean-spirited instigators. And sometimes they enlist me to play along, like during a three-game visit by the Florida Marlins. You see, when an expansion team is in town, the hijinks in the stands often beats the battle on the field. On this night of non-action on the diamond, a mischievous UPS group provided the entertainment for sections 416 and 417.

In that evening's outing, there were 30 United Parcel Service employees, twenty-eight male and two female. One of the two was with her spouse, the other was looking for the right guy. Or so the twenty-eight guys claimed.

One of these gentlemen (?) offered a twenty if I would put the old Bob charm to work. It was more like take it out of the attic and dust it off. The briber wanted me to engage in an animated conversation with her in a boisterous style so all her co-workers could hear, then ask for a date. With me, not for the guys she was with.

Well, I have scruples, values, and morals. I'd never humiliate someone in front of a group of peers. But it sounded like fun, the price was right, and she was a sizzling girl of summer. What was the worst that could happen?

I'd have a date. And even if I got shot down by her, at least if I could ham it up enough to entertain the people in the surrounding seats, I'd figure to make a bunch of additional beer sales.

So I straightened my cap, wiped the sweat from my brow, and removed the scum that forms on the lips' corners. Then I made my move on Shelley (all twenty-eight guys knew her name). Noticing that her cup was low on beer, I asked if I could fill her up with a tall boy. Oops, I had only twelve-ouncers in my tray. Either way, a cold one is a cold one and she was hot.

"And what's your story? What do you do for a living? Are any of these guys a brother, sheltering you from guys like me?" I was on a roll. Each line spoken heightened the theatrics with a crescendo effect.

With each new word out of my mouth, Shelley writhed in embarrassment. The seat was too small to hide under. The rest room not near enough. No sense stopping now. The onslaught continued.

"How often do you get to the games? Have you met any of the players? I know those guys. Can I tell you a thing or two about some of them. Maybe we can get together after the game at Brooklyn's Bar and Grill to have a cold one and I'll tell you some of those stories." Please note the operative word is story.

By now, associates sitting in front of her wore pained-poker faces so as not to ruin the gag. And those sitting behind gave up all hope of repressing a smile. They concerned themselves with stifling laughter.

A Season with Bob the Beerman

Realizing she had been set-up, Shelley suddenly launched a counter-attack. Catching everyone with their guard down, Shelley shot back, "Forget Brooklyn's. How about coming over to my place for a post-game cocktail?"

Jaws dropped like the sound of ice cubes into an empty drink glass. The UPS men were stunned. Silence gripped the section. Finally, one person muttered under his breath, "And all this time I never asked her out?"

"I'd love to," I answered without hesitation. "And I'll bring a bottle of Cabernet Sauvignon, on your friends," as I strolled up the aisle to collect a crisp twenty-dollar bill for my work.

A View from the Stands

WHAT ABOUT BOB?

The Kid doesn't chew tobacco, smoke, drink, curse, or chase broads. I don't see how he can possibly make it.
>   Richie Ashburn, broadcaster and leader of the lowly 1962 Mets

Fame wasn't something planned when I took the job as a beer vendor. It just happened. A spirit from above blessed me. Perhaps the same angel that blesses us each summer with baseball.

Of course, some believe people create their own destiny. Is it possible to be affected by both? What's the answer? I'm not positive. But this fleeing moment of glory sure is fun. As one fan put it, "Bob, you're the bright enema this town needed."

I'm still wondering exactly what he meant.

Another spectator suggested that I become the team's mascot. A Beerman as a mascot? In New York or Boston, it's a possibility. After all, in the east, the people socialize over food and drink and drink and drink. There's a strong connection between people, beer, and baseball.

But in the west, people fraternize over exercise and outdoor activity. Does that mean Yogi Bear should be the Colorado Rockies' mascot? Or how about Bob the Beerman?

Yet, some people think I'm just that. Just ask the people around town. I've heard the stories, and as the tales grow, so does the legend of Bob the Beerman.

One of my favorites was relayed to me by a fellow vendor, Ron Cobourn from Tucson. Seems like old "Sunburn Cobourn" was out painting the town Rockies' purple after a game one evening and sought alternative transportation home. He hailed a taxi, and soon was in a hometown baseball conversation with the driver. (Do people talk about anything other than the Rockies in this city?)

The driver recognized Sunburn as a hot dog vendor at the stadium.

"Do you know Bob the Beerman?" asked the taxi operator. "He's great to bat the breeze with. And he's my personal beerman!"

Definitely a sign of celebrity status, when you're a taxi driver's hero. Think of the cross-section of people he's in contact with, the movie stars, politicians, and athletes. And yet, one of his proudest acquaintances is Bob the Beerman.

Wonder if I'm the biggest celebrity he's met? Feel pretty certain I'm at least ranked ahead of former Vice-President Dan Quayle.

I've got to find out his badge and license number. That way, I'll know I'll have a private chauffeur around the metro area.

Then there was the nightly news appearance. NBC-TV wanted to do a feature piece on Bob before one afternoon game, to be shown during that evening's news broadcast.

Well, I spent an hour in make-up, two hours in wardrobe, and three hours filming. All that for a measly ninety seconds of air time. I'll tell you, Hollywood is sure tough!

Radio work isn't much easier. There's no make-up or costume involved, but I sure had to be careful what I said. A big radio network, I don't remember if it was National Public Radio or Radio Free America, miked me during one ball game. Then they played out-takes from my dialogue during the morning rush hour drive shows. Fortunately, I kept all the interaction clean. Remember, I run a family show.

A fan did have some choice words for me though. Turns out he awoke one morning to my banter blaring on his clock radio. That evening at the park, he said to me, "Bob, you're like a bad dream. You won't go away. Your voice is the last one I hear at night when I leave the stadium, and it's the first thing I hear in the morning. How about I buy you a one-way plane ticket somewhere?"

A View from the Stands

Another media-type event I was involved in was a marriage proposal. Found out, unfortunately after the fact, that a very eligible and attractive female anchorperson was going to pop the question to me.

But just before she had the chance, the television station's legal expert proposed on air to her. Not to publicly embarrass the made-for-TV lawyer, she accepted, leaving heartbroken Bob outside, looking in.

And in Colorado's mountainous ski resort towns, Bob has become a pop icon. In recognition of both his skiing talents and beerman personna, the town of Avon throws an annual Bobfest on Memorial Day weekend. Other lesser Bob's that have appeared include those with surnames Hope and Newhart.

In addition, the hamlet has a bridge named after me. It's called Bob's Bridge. Then again, I've seen my name Bob inscribed on the sides of many bridges throughout the country.

A Season with Bob the Beerman

Lean, Mean, Fighting Machines

We're not athletes. We're baseball players.
John Kruk, Phillie first baseman

" Tired of getting sand kicked in your face? Try 'Bodies by Charles Atlas'."

Remember that advertisement from the back pages of cheap magazines in the 1960's and '70's?? If not, trust me, those ads did exist. You're just too young to recall.

The current generation of ballplayers evidently never read those publications, as more than a handful could use the help of Chuck. Some major leaguers are closer in appearance to Jellyroll Morton than to the Man of Steel. In this era of million-dollar salaries, more than one of these rich kids is on a dime store diet. Some of the fattest contracts belong, perhaps appropriately, to the fattest players (doughboys?). Every levee along the Mississippi could have been plugged with the baseball members to Oprah's Overweight Organization.

Ok, ok, so I've been unnecessarily harsh. But let's be serious for a moment. If you had an opportunity to make a seven-figure salary for five or six years, but it depended upon how well you performed in a physical activity (well, baseball is a more physically exhausting sport than golf), wouldn't you want to be in prime condition to maximize your performance and earnings over a relatively short career???

Ballplayers aren't any more out of shape than the general population, you argue? Look at the crowd in any stadium, you say.

A View from the Stands

For every person with whippet-like thinness, there's one with a body as lifeless as a beached humpback. How many times have you had to sit next to a person who bought one ticket but filled two-and-a-half seats?

But these plumplings aren't being paid fourteen jigga-million dollars to play a sport, I'd like to point out. Besides, it's you, the fan, who is forking over the bucks to support these athletes (?) who belong to the Body by Budweiser Club.

With that in mind, here's an All-Pillsbury team of Major Leaguers you definitely don't want to invite to Thanksgiving Dinner, unless your mother-in-law is cooking. In that case, let them eat first, and you'll be spared both the indigestion and the leftovers.

Starting in the outfield for this team of misfits - at least in their uniforms, with the beer-barrel body and signature pout, is Kevin Mitchell of the Cincinnati Reds. Despite the expanding waist-line and body so often injured it's held together by duct tape, Mitchell can still hit the ball. That is, when a sore _____ (put any body part in the blank) doesn't keep him out of the line-up.

Tony Gwynn of San Diego is the second participant in the outfield that covers no ground. The only talented individual of the lowly Padres, he's won more batting titles than his team has won games. Well, almost. This, despite being shaped like a bowling pin after a few too many strikes. A class guy in a classless organization, you're tempted to buy him a membership to the nearest Jack LaLane Spa.

Rounding out the outfield is the Minnesota Twins' Kirby Puckett. He's surprisingly agile for a person who's circumference nearly matches his height. The consummate team player, the Big Bucket turned down millions of dollars to stay in Minnesota.

In the infield, the Philadelphia Phillies' John Kruk anchors first base. I'm sure he could probably anchor the Queen Mary too. Some contend that his twin brother is the Phillie Phanatic, a round mound of green-globbed fuzz that's the Phillies' mascot. Both are hairy, move with a limping gait, and dress in the polyester tradition. But the Phanatic is better looking. That's ok, because the Krukster has consistently been among the National League batting

A Season with Bob the Beerman

leaders.

At second base is Mark Lemke of the Atlanta Braves. He made it not so much because of his physical attributes. He's only 175 pounds soaking wet, with a full stomach. He's on the squad because of his name. A Lemke sounds like some type of slow, pudgy, sloth-toed, crustacean.

Bobby Bonilla plays third base for this squad that more closely resembles a beer-league slo-pitch softball team, which is synonymous with the New York Mets. The Metsies happen to be Bonilla's team. Ground balls hit to third are often lost in the eclipse caused by his girth.

Pitching is Fernando Valenzuela of the Baltimore Orioles. He throws left-handed and eats right-handed, so even on the mound food is never out of reach. The former Dodger great from south of the border pretends not to speak English when asked his weight.

Holding down the backstop position is Detroit Tiger Mickey Tettleton. He catches not only curves and sliders, but also half-eaten popcorn boxes, peanut shells, and hot dog wrappers blowing across the diamond. One teammate said Tettleton takes these home to use in a stew.

Wheww!

Being a knowledgeable baseball fan, you probably noticed that there's no shortstop on the All-Pillsbury team. Sorry, I searched and hunted and bent the rules, but couldn't find one to meet specifications. It's impossible to find a fat shortstop. The two words aren't compatible. Just like the words "power-hitting shortstop."

But there's other weighty matters on my mind. Like, when the fat lady sings, should it be the national anthem, or when this team's ball game is history??

Look out John Madden, my All-Pillsbury team is ready to challenge your All-Madden squad to a true test of athletic ability. Say lawn darts at fifteen paces??

Editor's note: Please note, the above players change teams about as often as they eat. Any of the above could be on a new team as you read this. Any of them could have lost weight too.

A View from the Stands

FICKLE FANS' BILL OF RIGHTS

Some day, I would like to go up in the stands and boo some fans.

Bo Belinsky, former Angel pitcher

Wrigley Field has its Bleacher Bums, Yankee Stadium has its Bronx Zoo, and the Colorado Rockies have The Rockpile. Alcatraz was a safer place than these enclaves of enraged fans. And, unfortunately, not all the whacko's masquerading as baseball fans will sit in the psycho sections. Yes, Jason escaped and he could be in the chair next to you!!

This is where the creepy, spooky music would come in if this were a slasher movie instead of a baseball book.

Along with admission to the ballpark, which costs Joe Fanatic one, two, or fifty dollars, comes certain inalienable rights. These were designed by our nation's founding fathers and included in the Bill of Rights. Or so Joe Fanatic claims.

With a "Body by Haagen-Daaz" and enough back hair to weave a toupee for his thinly-veiled head, Joe Fanatic insists on the right to bare arms, chest, and legs, peeling his shirt and oiling his lard. The people occupying seats near him insist on the right to maintain cans of Deep Woods Off and Lysol Spray to de-bug and disinfect the surrounding environment.

These prove worthless. Only a nuclear meltdown could destroy the odors and animals emanating from the tropical rain forest growing on Joe's back.

Protection from illegal search and seizure is another right Joe Fanatic declares as he enters the stadium. You, me, and everyone else know Joe will attempt to smuggle in enough booze to intoxi-

A Season with Bob the Beerman

cate a small, South Pacific nation, or at least four Soviet sailors.

But Joe knows his rights. He purposely subjects himself to a search at the stadium gate. There, the security patrol find on his body two cans of cheap Meisterbrau beer and an airline-sized bottle of Bacardi. These are seized, and Joe is allowed to proceed.

Well, the beers were a plant. Joe only drinks imports. And the bottle of rum was a decoy - actually filled with water. His water bottle, which went through unscathed, contained the Bacardi 151.

So there's no need for Joe to buy beer in the stadium. He saves his bucks and purchases Coca-Cola to mix with the rum. No worry about being flagged by a beerman.

But one day Joe Fanatic was flagged by a Coke vendor. Vendor #0036 Peddlin' Pat Haywood cut-off soda sales to Joe due to excessive belligerence.

Seems like Mr. Fanatic was riding Peddlin' about the warm soda, the soggy cups, and the high price. Turns out Pat is usually a beer vendor. He deals with drunks in the stands all the time. Just kidding about drunks in the stadium Mr. Mayor and Mr. ARA Services. Number 0036 wasn't going to take any grief from a toasted Joe Fanatic, so he cut him off from any more soda. And as Peddlin' swung his arm in the universal bartender's No-More-You've-Had-Too-Many sign, he conveniently knocked over and spilled the open water bottle filled with rum.

Another article on Joe Fanatic's Bill of Rights is freedom of speech. Joe believes that his ticket empowers him to be a blustery talk show persona, with the stadium as his studio. He knows more about nothing than you and me know about anything. That's no put down to us either. Would you be proud to brag about knowing much of nothing?? Joe is.

And more than once Joe has shown his wisdom parallels his knowledge of nothing.

Take the time Joe weaseled his way into some prime seats behind the third base dugout. From this vantage point, Joe was within earshot of the players' on-field conversations. So Joe invoked the freedom of speech act. No topic was closed for discussion. Body parts, ancestry, and lifestyles all were fair

A View from the Stands

game for Joe.

It was the Reds and the Rockies playing the game, and Joe and his insults trashed everyone's name.

That was until the fourteenth inning or so, when Rob Dibble of Cincinnati took the ball into his hands. Ok, so Dibble is a pitcher. Naturally he's going to take the ball into his hands.

For those of you who know something about baseball players, there's a term for those with an elevator that doesn't go to the top floor. It's called flake. Using this to describe Dibble would be considered a complement. A sabre-toothed tiger with a paramecium's mind would be closer to reality.

Only joking there, Rob. (Just in case he reads this book.)

But Joe wasn't aware of Dibble's volatility.

With the Reds batting in the top of some extra-inning, Dibble sauntered into the on-deck circle. Riding the Reds' pitcher like a barnstormer in an air show, Joe Fanatic was merciless.

"Dibble, you stink, you crazed animal. You're ugly. You're a bum!"

Having heard enough of the trash-talking, Dibble suddenly rose and turned toward the grandstand where Joe was located. With a glare that froze ice, Dibble said, "What game are you watching? I've shut your team out over the last four innings on one-hit ball. Have another beer. Better yet, get a life!"

Did this episode change Joe? Of course not.

You see, Joe has a disease called Beer-Bias. Don't know if this term is in Webster's Dictionary, so I'll give you the bartender's and beerman's definition. Beer-Bias is when the magical brew affects physical, intellectual, and emotional processes. Sub-species of this is beer-bladder, beer-balls, and beer-hormones.

Beer-Bias' physical effects are beer-bladder. That's when Joe Fanatic consumes more hops and barley than his body can store. And Joe doesn't heed his body's physical needs. Can't put a twelve-pack in a six-pack carrier. Joe is too much of a lazy load to visit the latrine. He fills the damn to its crest before draining the dragon. It's safer to stand in front of a charging bronco than it is to be in the path of Joe's mad dash.

Beer-balls are the intellectual effects of Beer-Bias. More

specifically, the non-intellectual effects. Like after filling the damn, suddenly Joe wants to take on Godzilla in hand-to-hand combat. Or worse still, he challenges a nose-guard from a renegade college football program to a best two-out-of-three fall sumo wrestling match.

Joe feels much mightier when he gets a case of the beer-balls.

Beer-hormones kick-in after Joe wets himself, and has his nose relocated forty-five degrees west of his right ear lobe. Beer-hormones tell Joe to make a move on the hottest babe spotted while his vision is still functional. Or on anything he thought resembled a woman after losing use of his eyeballs. This loss of vision is due to either too much beer or leading with his face too often against the nose-tackle.

Of course, beer-hormones only work in the movies. And this isn't Hollywood, it's reality.

And in real life, Joe leaves the stadium at the end of the night the same way he arrived. Alone and out of it.

A View from the Stands

FOOT POWER

This guy is so old that the first time he had athlete's foot, he used Absorbine Sr.
        Bob Costas as an NBC sportscaster

Like the bison in the Old West, vendors have free roam of the ball yard's fertile feeding grounds. Scaling the heights or down in the lowlands like the plains Indians of a century ago, the hawker leads a nomadic existence across the stadium's expanses.
    STOP!
    Enough of this local color horse____! You're not writing a tribute to the Sioux Indians, the frontiersmen settling new lands, or Lewis and Clark and the Oregon Trail.
    You're writing about people's feet! That's right, five digits attached to a couple of bones, wrapped in a slab of flesh.
    Face it, you just had no clue how to start this piece, so you began with romantic embellishment! How else could you expect someone to read this??
    Ok, ok, I admit to the crime. I plead guilty. Please don't confiscate my literary license. I promise this article will smell as sweet as a mountain spring shower. Ok, that may be a reach, but just read a bit more. I swear you'll enjoy it!
    You see, as a vendor, sometimes we're down close to action, only a penny's pitch from the field. From there, we hear the umpire bellowing the balls and strikes and see the contorted facial expressions of the third base coach relaying the signs to the batter.
    For most beermen, these are only fleeing moments. We spend our time eyeing the crowd, seeking a taker for our tonic. And

A Season with Bob the Beerman

when a buyer beckons, we spring to action.
   Back to the field,
   down to a knee,
   pouring a beer,
   feet's all we see.
   That's right folks.
   Feet.
   Better than fifty percent of our time is spent eye-level with feet. If we're doing our job, we're
   crouched on a knee,
   facing the fan,
   selling some beer,
   emptying a can.
   Ok, I promise, no more bad rhymes.
   You get the picture. Vendors see more feet than Imelda Marcos has shoes. To us, each row is a centipede.
   We see all types of feet. Bozo the Clown versions, and those that fit into a glass slipper. Those with bunions, hammer-toes, corns, and callouses. Athletes' feet and athlete's foot. Some are diseased with mildewy metatarsus, foot fungus, and toe-jam; others finely pedicured by a Beverly Hills' salon. Some appear gnawed with dying, dirt-filled toenails as jagged as a tiger shark's tooth, while others are just nailless, like a snail outside its shell.
   STOP!
   This is nauseous. My stomach's churning. I'm ruining my appetite.
   Let's face reality. Bare feet are gross! Simple as that.
   As a beer vendor stuck with part-time foot patrol, I'd issue citations to any individual wearing sandals, Tevas, Birkenstocks, or open-toed shoes.
   I would not serve them a beer. I would not let them in my house. I would not let them pass Go and collect two hundred dollars.
   I'll take a young couple in Italian designer footwear any time. He in hand-sewn Gucci loafers, she in Enzo flats. No bare feet here. Polished-to-perfection and squeaky-clean, they probably own a Ferrari. This twosome has class. I'd serve them Dom Perignon in crystal champagne flutes from a sterling silver tray.

A View from the Stands

I'm selling out, you say? Bob the Beerman, a working class stiff, mixing with the socialites, catering to the Lord Wennington Smythe III's of the world?

Hey, young couples sporting fancy foreign footwear tip well. Believe me, I know from experience. Like, "Here's a fifty, keep the change."

Anyone wearing shoes more expensive than my car has bucks. I'm not bashful about taking their money. I view it as equitable compensation for all the sickly feet I see every day. Hazard pay if you will.

As a matter of fact, there's a whole tipping scale based on footwear.

At the top are the imports. Not even close here. Just refer to the case of Lord Wennington.

Next come the wing-tips. Businessmen closing business transactions at the ballpark. If the deal is done, definitely some coin for the beerman in this action.

Boat shoes, penny-loafers, and ultra-white cross-trainers. All are a slice of Americana. These people tip like the cross-section of the population that they are, average but fair.

Running shoes and hiking boots. Hit and miss here. If it's Olympic Marathon champion Frank Shorter in a pair of Nike, you'll see some coin. Is that what you wear, Frank? Apologize to your shoe sponsor for me if it's not. And have him send me a pair or two. I go through a couple sets a season.

World class athletes have world class endorsement contracts. The tip they give the beerman may be in running clothes, but at today's prices it beats a George or an Abe.

The flip side of the coin is if it's an armchair athlete wearing his lawn-mowing hiking boots - good luck.

Cowboy boots. Brand new genuine imitation snakeskin western boots with synthetic leather uppers and a high-gloss shine - a tourist making a first visit to Colorado. They came to view the Rockies, Mountains that is, not the baseball team. No way you'll get anything out of them.

Well-worn, prairie dust-covered, with cow chips clinging to the boot bottoms - a real big sky cowpoke here. Redman chewing tobacco sends them Christmas cards. Hard-working, they value

A Season with Bob the Beerman

the money earned at some of the toughest labor around. Get them a shot of Jack Daniels to go along with a Bud, and they'll take care of you for life.

The open-shoed and the shoeless. Please see above. My stomach can't handle writing another paragraph about that.

A View from the Stands

WHAT DO YOU DO IN REAL LIFE?

Little League baseball is a very good thing because it keeps the parents off the streets.

Yogi Berra, whose Yankee uniform has been retired

Crime fighter by day, Budman by night! It's Bob the Beerman!

For most vendors, daytime isn't as eventful. Like a statistical sampling of working people in the general population with a standard deviation of plus or minus two confidence intervals as determined by linear regression analysis, each vendor is a random variable dispersed about a scatter diagram in inverse correlation to his day job. Got that?

In other words, what any hawker does by day is not necessarily reflected by his personality once the vending uniform goes on.

Sorry about all the statistical lingo above. I asked one of the vending boss big-wigs at ARA Services, Charlie Levering (a.k.a. Mr. Freon - for his always calm, cool demeanor) for a list of the vendors' names and badge numbers. He gave me a computer print-out containing more numbers and information than a Pentagon defense budget. Felt I should make it sound like I actually used his list, even though it's lining the bottom of my bird cage.

So what are some of the real life occupations of those providing seat-side service with a stadium smile?

A group belong to the education field. They're either still in school, figuring some way to get out of school, or never graduated from school. And can you believe people actually trust us to make

A Season with Bob the Beerman

change?

Really, it's not that bad. ARA taught us how to use our toes if we ran out of fingers to figure how little change is returned to the customer.

Boy, this is starting to sound like David Letterman dissing his old corporate officers at NBC and GE.

In reality, there are some educators in the crew. Dan "Lucky 13" O'Brien (vendor #13) works with physically and emotionally disabled students. The bearded-wonder also vended for the three-time World Series champion Oakland A's during the early seventies.

Jeff Moore "Beer" (#79), another of the bearded-scholarly types, has one year to retirement from high school. Not as a student, as a teacher. Then he plans to go on the professional vendors' tour. If his wife permits.

John "Coach" Nelson (#14) is a retired college coach. Retired at 44? Come on, John, which NCAA rule did your team violate?? Gramps, as he's affectionately known, coached the fishing team at East Florida Panhandle South Community College and Grill. He also led the school's night crawler expedition.

And Michael "The Professor" Greenholz (#130) is a college English instructor. An Italian boy from Long Island, New York, with Tony Danza looks, I bet he gets all the long, blond-hair, cheerleader-type coeds.

All right, so he has a Jewish surname. It makes for a better story line if he's Italian. It's the only way I can use the Tony Danza analogy. Oh, yeh, he's also editing this book, so if there's something in it you don't like, Michael is listed in the yellow pages and can be contacted at that number.

There's also some aspiring, or perhaps perspiring students in the nighttime huckster role. Rod Vanderwall (#231, formerly #568 -he got a promotion) is studying energy conservation and completing his master's thesis.

Still.

Just don't ask what decade he started it.

Energy conservation, hmm, maybe I should volunteer to help out. I could be a case study. Two full-leafed aspen trees. Hammock. Shade. A cold one. Energy conservation right there.

65

A View from the Stands

There are the professionally-employed moonlighting as vendors. Bill "Side" Burns (#169) is an attorney. In his spare time, Counselor handles all accident liability cases occurring in the stadium.

And then there are the mysteriously-employed. No one is quite sure what a handful of the guys do by day. Like "Jumpin'" Gerry Halpin (#46). Undergrad from University of Virginia, MBA from University of Colorado, sitting on a bunch of stock options after a power play at his company.

Ladies, here's a catch. Single, well-educated, diverse financial portfolio, and a beerman. What else can you ask for??

There are diamond men, beer men, and earth men by day, wearing vendor stripes by night. Terry Hammen "Eggs" (#131) and Paul Etchegoinberry (#177) - that's his real name, no nickname required - are jewelers in real life. Get your Batman decoder rings there.

Eric Beermann (#156) isn't a beer distributor by day. With a name like that, he ought to be. He vended 165 straight days one season with the Chicago Cubs, White Sox, and Bulls. He's the Ironman of the Professional Vendors' Tour.

And Earthman (#8), well, he's just earth, man. He's the resident ballpark bratwurst baron, the only vendor selling these in the entire stadium. His kids even call him Earthman. Oh, yeah, his real name is Brent Doeden. I only discovered in the last few minutes while writing this piece.

And how about Leather Teddy. No, don't ask for it. That's another vendor. Ted Altenritter (#23) specializes in 'Designs in Fine Leather', as his business card states. He covers everything in leather, from shoes to purses to hats. He even redesigned Bo Jackson's multi-purpose, two-sport, hand-sewn, baseball-batting, football-receiving gloves.

Then there's "Vending" Vince DiLorenzo (#201), a former mortgage broker in California, who relocated to a new state to take advantage of unsuspecting first-time home buyers, though he unequivocally denies it.

And what about Bob (#1)?

No, I'm not a used car salesman, nor do I drive a Good Humor Ice Cream truck. I live in The People's Republic of

A Season with Bob the Beerman

Boulder. I play by day.

Wiffle ball, that is, with the neighborhood kids. I'm the commissioner, the home run leader, the best pitcher, and the rules maker. I run Bob's Backyard Whiffle Ball League like Capone ran the mob from cell block "C."

That is, when I'm not undertaking household chores like the laundry. Ever notice every single article of clothing removed from the dryer is turned inside-out and tied into some Mongolian strangler knot? Not even a six-year-old struggling to remove his Toughskin blue jeans without first removing his sneakers could get the clothes that discombobulated.

Must be some type of creature inhabiting the dryer which specializes in tying clothes into non-human knots. So I spend a great deal of time unbinding my shorts and other duds.

Eventually, I throw in the towel at untangling the laundry and just shove the ball of clothes into the linen closet. Then I tool around my house pretending to be Tim Allen of *Home Improvement* fame. It's scary, being so unskilled at household repairs, that the inept Mr. Allen is a role model.

And I am slowly approaching Tim's level of craftsmanship. I've mastered two tools, and am close to besting a third.

Figured out how to use a crowbar pretty quickly, only took three or four classes.

Next came the duct tape. Took about as long to disentangle and conqueror as it did unleashing a woman's bra for the first time.

As soon as I determine how to unlock the vise grips from my shirt sleeve, I'll be ready to fix anything.

The kid next door, Dennis Mitchell, already has his friends calling me good, old, Mr. Wilson.

A View from the Stands

STADIUM SOCIAL STATUS

When the Yankees go out for dinner, they reserve twenty-five tables for one.
Anonymous

The federal government has an endless array of classifications for the citizens of this great country.
Demographically speaking, at any moment in time, you or I may be one of the following colors (choose one): a) white b) black c) brown d) yellow e) green f) pink g) mauve.

We may be of the following ethnic groups (choose one or more): a) African American b) Native American c) South American d) European American f) Asian American g) Non-American h) New Yorker i) other.

And, given the Reagan-Bush years, we may be of the following income class (choose one that most approximately represents your position): a) poverty level b) lower c) low d) somewhat low e) almost middle f) middle g) just above middle h) super-duper filthy-rich above upper class.

It's the same at the ballpark.
A class system also exists.
Think about it for a second.
On any night, there's 50,000-some people at the stadium, each from a unique walk-of-life. Each from different jobs, lifestyles, and social structures.

Add to that all the ball yard support workers required to make the game come off and run smoothly. Suddenly, there's a demographic cross-section of America that the boys in Washington would love to use as a statistical sampling.

A Season with Bob the Beerman

Sorry, guys, I beat you to it. I'm using them for my Inaugural Unofficial Occupational Class Study of Individuals at a Ball Game.

You see, my theory is, ummh, err, aaah . . . . Well, just keep reading, and I'm sure I'll come up with something. And it will make a heck of a lot more sense than some hypothesis derived by a dozen D.C. men hidden in a double-top-secret location wearing white shirts with soup-stained ties and poly-prophylactic pocket protectors using Venn Diagrams, super computers, and self-sharpening pencils.

And to think, I just draw my conclusions in the dirt like a quarterback of a sandlot football game.

The first thing is to group people by type of profession. For our classification purposes, fans and stadium support employees will start in the same hopper. From there, we'll differentiate by job category, then rank these according to socioeconomic status.

Got that?

If not, contact your tax accountant. If she can understand the biggest of the big Federal bureaucracies (the IRS, dummy), she will comprehend my simplistic status system.

By what professions should the crowd be classified? Well, at any game, there are doctors, lawyers, accountants, engineers, construction workers, cowboys and farmers, and retailers.

My apologies if you don't fit into any of those categories. Get a real job.

And now to classify the stadium personnel. There's security, maintenance, food servers, grounds keepers, and journalists. And of course, vendors and ballplayers.

With that done, let's start to determine the socioeconomic status system.

Leading off are the doctors and lawyers.

Surprised here?

No way. All earn lots and lots of money.

But that's just the economic side. What about social status?

Well, consider this. Scientists have begun using lawyers instead of rats for lab tests. There are certain things even a rat won't do. And aren't doctors really scientists? They both wear white medical jackets and take educated guesses at the correct diagnosis. So doctors and the lawyers hang-out together.

Got the connection between doctors, scientists, and lawyers? If not, it's still probably clearer than anything a doctor, lawyer, or scientist ever said to you. At least they provide a good base for our class system. Someone has to be at the bottom.

One step above are the stadium maintenance personnel. They take out the trash and fix clogged toilets, but enjoy what they are doing. More power to them for job satisfaction, but it's hard to rank anyone who plays in the sewer much higher than just above doctors and lawyers.

Next up the scale are journalists. Bad wardrobes, bad hair styles, bad writing, bad socioeconomic position.

A dead heat exists at the next level in the status classes between accountants and engineers. Both are heavily into numbers.

No, I don't mean the type Michael Jordan and Pete Rose were into. Too bad they weren't into those kind of numbers, at least the number-crunchers-for-a-profession would be more interesting to converse with at cocktail hour.

People in these professions are characterized by conservative, out-of-date clothing styles and haircuts just a trim better than those of journalists. And they are not bad writers. They just can't form complete sentences. This gives them the edge over the media-types.

Food servers hold the next class. Without these people, we'd all be hungry. They help keep us happy by filling our stomachs. I like food. I like these people.

Just ahead on the socioeconomic ladder are security personnel. They protect us. Hmmm, my stomach just won out over my need for safety. Flip-flop food servers and security people in the standings.

At the next level are the construction workers and stadium grounds keepers. Both toil in the soil, aren't afraid to get dirty, and work with Mother Earth. Anyone who takes care of the good Mother should be held in high esteem. They sacrifice money for the betterment of everyone on the planet.

Reaching the upper echelons of the status scale are the cowboys and farmers. Combining the best of the food servers,

A Season with Bob the Beerman

construction workers, and grounds keepers, they cultivate the land and raise food. Only thing holding them back from even greater prestige is that both cowboys and farmers work with manure.

Near the top are retailers.

Hang on one second, while I try to remember why they are rated this highly.

I think it's because most of the retailers I know are all well-dressed, stunningly attractive females driving fast cars. I'm only human. Even the government's demographic studies have biases.

At the top, naturally, are the ballplayers. They get paid megabucks - even more than doctors and lawyers, travel around the country, work three hours a day for six months, and have lots of free time. Utopia.

Oops, maybe the players aren't quite at the zenith of the socioeconomic scale.

You see, vendors are.

Vendors get paid to be at the game. Fans have to pay to be there.

Vendors leave with $50 or $100 more than what they came. Fans leave with $50 to $100 less in their pockets.

Vendors are sought by more people during the game than the ballplayers.

And vendors don't have to worry about being bumped into a higher tax bracket like the millionaire players.

A View from the Stands

WHAT I REALLY MEANT WAS . . .

I think too much on the mound sometimes, and get brain cramps.

          Britt Burns, as a White Sox pitcher

Ever been asked something really dumb? Something so stupid that you clamped down the molars into your tongue with such force that your eyes watered? It was the only way to prevent some snide retort.

So how do you handle these mindless questions? Is there any way to avoid them? Wouldn't it be easier if you could just administer some local anesthesia to these people? Perhaps like the Three Stooges with an oversized wooden hammer to the lame brain's head? Boink!

At the ballpark, us vendors see, know, and hear all.

Mr. Matchbook was trying to light Mrs. Candlestick's fire? Ooops, that one slipped. You didn't really hear that gossip here, right?

And we have to show patience towards the fans' questions, comments, and quips. No matter how asinine, stupid, or boorish.

So, how do we, the beer man, hot dog guy, and the peanut person cope??

We reply with an appropriately uniform, courteous answer to the lout's, I mean, customer's question. But as our tongues' produce the politically correct response, our minds are running with a cutting comment which we would like to use as our comeback.

A Season with Bob the Beerman

To the fans' frivolous inquiries, here are some of the standard vendor remarks, followed by the snappy retorts that are running through our minds and would just love to say. And I'm sure you would love to hear.

Fan says: Is the beer cold?
Vendor replies: Ice cold, sir.
Vendor thinks: No, I'm test marketing a new type of beer, a warmer-than-room-temperature variety brewed from food scraps clogging my garbage disposal. And besides, you had so many before arriving at the stadium, I could pass-off bat urine in a beer can as a brewski to you .

Fan says: Do you have _____ (put any ballpark food here that the vendor is not carrying)?
Vendor replies: Sorry, sir, I'm not handling that today.
Vendor thinks: Open your #@$%& eyes! Does it look like that's what I have?? What does the lettering on the vending tray read?? Have you noticed the buttons pinned to my shirt that spell out the products and prices of the goods I'm carrying??

Fan says: Where are the nearest rest rooms?
Vendor replies: Just up on the concourse.
Vendor thinks: Right where you're sitting. No one will notice. There's already spilled liquids under your seat.

Fan says: Do you have napkins?
Vendor says: Sorry, just ran out.
Vendor thinks: Do I look like the paper goods' aisle at the supermarket? This is a ballpark. Everyone leaves with mustard stains on their clothes.

Fan says: Is this my right section?
Vendor replies: Let me check your ticket. Hmmm. You should be over three more aisles.
Vendor thinks: Is this an usher uniform I'm wearing?!? No! You should be glad I didn't banish you to the south stands, you snake, trying to weasel your way into better seats.

A View from the Stands

Fan says: Can you break a hundred dollar bill?
Vendor replies: It should be no problem, sir.
Vendor thinks: I'd like to break it over your head. A hundred dollar bill for a $1.25 red rope! What am I, Citibank?? Why don't you just ask your five-year-old son for money. He probably has exact change, with a tip to boot.

Fan says: Where can I get a program?
Vendor replies: Up on the concourse, sir. (A pat answer to any stadium-related query.)
Vendor thinks: Don't give me that now-I-have-to-walk-all-the-way-back-up-there look. You were the bonehead that didn't purchase one before reaching your seats. And no, I'm not making a special delivery to chase one down for you.

Fan says: How do I get an autograph?
Vendor replies: You have to be at field level along the railing during batting practice.
Vendor thinks: With a pencil and paper. And I can get you some. Matter of fact, I'll do them myself. Whose do you want?? John, Paul, George, and Ringo's? Charlie Manson? Jack the Ripper? James Garfield? Who's that, you ask? The 20th President of the United States.

Fan says: Do you accept tips?
Vendor replies: If you deem the service acceptable.
Vendor thinks: No, that's ok, I don't need the money. It's probably better spent if it's put towards the car payments on your Jaguar or the mortgage on your Key Largo beach house. I don't have a car loan. My 1971 Volkswagen Beetle is paid off. And I live in a two-bedroom apartment with my wife and five almost-college-age children. No home-funding problems here.

Fan says: Do you have Zima?
Vendor replies: Sorry, it's only available at the Beers of the World stands on the concourse.
Vendor thinks: Do I look like I'd be carrying Zima? Only real beer here. I request to be disbarred from the vending fraternity and

A Season with Bob the Beerman

executed at twelve paces if I ever, ever, ever am forced to sell that stuff.

Fan says: How am I supposed to drink this soda without a straw?
Vendor replies: Well, you might start by removing the lid.
Vendor thinks: Life's tough when you're stupid. It's tougher when your IQ doubled equals the ERA of an expansion team's bullpen.

Fan says: Do you have Diet Coke?
Vendor replies: Sorry, I carry only the fattening stuff.
Vendor thinks: No, but I'll gladly pour half of it in your lap. That way you'll only drink half the calories of a regular Coke.

Fan says: Why are peanuts three dollars?
Vendor replies: I guess it's the laws of supply and demand.
Vendor thinks: 'Cause someone is ripping you off. Besides, I hear part of the money goes to the Jimmy Carter Ex-President Fund. After all, he's building homes in third world countries now.

Fan says: Where's Bob the Beerman?
Vendor (other than Bob) replies: Bob doesn't work here any more. He doesn't need the money. He won the lottery and moved to Monte Carlo.
Vendor (other than Bob) thinks: What a marketing scam-artist Bob is. At least now all his loyal customers think he's gone, and they will buy from me!

A View from the Stands

FREEBIES, PROMOTIONS, AND GIVEAWAYS

About this autograph business. Once, someone in Washington sent up a picture to me and I wrote, 'Do good in school.' I look up, this guy is seventy-eight years old.
   Casey Stengel, legendary Yankee and Met manager

When stores advertise "Special! Limited Time Only!", "Deep Discounts!", and "Buy One! - Get One Free!" deals, the savvy shopper's initial reaction is, "I've gotta get down there first thing when the doors open." The second thought is, "I wonder what's wrong. Business must be bad."

Around the major leagues, all teams sponsor promotional games. Giveaways run the gamut from batting glove day to cap night. Some teams schedule special events for 78 of the 81 home dates. The business manager gets three floating holidays. That's why there's no freebies for three of the games.

With all these specials offered to attract customers, does that mean professional baseball is in financial peril? If it's the San Diego Padres, you bet. If it's the New York Mets, it's not economic ruin, but rather on-field woes.

These special promotional days (vs. regular promotional days - anybody know the difference?) are intended to generate additional revenue for the home team by spurring fan interest. Or attracting them to the ballpark in hopes that they'll spend lavishly. Or enticing people to watch the game on television, view the commercials, and buy the sponsors' products - which means more advertising dollars to the television station - which means higher

A Season with Bob the Beerman

rights fees for the home team.

Usually, the money brought into the team's coffers on a promotional event exceeds the outlay for the souvenir or post-game entertainment.

Usually.

Sometimes it doesn't. Sometimes promotional events are so ill-conceived you'd swear it was the Junior Assistant Bookkeeper in Charge of Green, Six-Column Ledger Paper who developed the idea instead of the Senior Executive Vice-President and Director of Marketing in Charge of Nothing.

Here are some of the best, or in this case, worst, promotional events. Some actually happened, some we'd like to see happen, and some are just waiting to happen.

Chicago, the late 1970's. Saturday Night Fever fever was sweeping the nation. John Travolta and the disco rage was the pop culture. Between games of a Chicago White Sox doubleheader, a local radio station sponsored a disco destruction night at the ballpark. Bring a disco record to the stadium, get a discount ticket to the game, and donate the "Best of the Bee Gees" to the World's Largest Exploding Disco Album Collection.

A drunken, rowdy crowd, the largest of the season to see the hapless Pale Hose, quickly became bored with the on-field play. Armed with LP's and 45's, the fans soon realized they could entertain themselves with the records while waiting for disco detonation.

Close-and-Play phonographs weren't required. The fans took to flinging the discs across the stands. Albums were raining down throughout ancient Comiskey Park. Ultimate Frisbee was given a new meaning.

Black vinyl filled the air in an explosive environment. As the first game neared completion, the hooliganism worsened. Night fever swept the air. Fans were just trying to "Stayin' Alive."

Crowd control was lost.

During the first game, ushers attempted to collect the albums. Some were confiscated, most weren't. Between games, all the records were placed into an over-sized wooden coffin, to signify the death of disco music. A few sticks of dynamite were wired to the crate and detonated, sending vinyl shrapnel sky-high.

77

A View from the Stands

Chaos ensued.
The field was littered with disco records, some destroyed, most not. Fans rampaged in drunken disorder. Authorities were unable to restore civility. The second game of the doubleheader was canceled, a forfeit victory awarded to the visiting team. An innocent promotion had turned into an ugly incident of random, uncontrolled actions by intoxicated fans.

The Bronx, New York, early 1980's. Bat Day at Yankee Stadium - the final chapter.

Distributing 12,000 wooden baseball bats to all youths in attendance under the age of 16.

In the South Bronx. A neighborhood where drug dealers and criminals earn more respect than parents, teachers, and police officers.

Inner-city, under-privileged people.

Burned-out, graffiti-covered buildings.

Ethnic diversity, racial differences. Summertime tensions to match summertime heat. Violent demonstrations, gang riots.

Lawlessness.

Almost a 50% high school drop-out rate. Instead of carrying text books, kids tote semi-automatic guns, hunting knives, and tire chains.

And the Yankees held the Bat Day promotion. Another weapon for thousands of youths who spend their evenings pillaging the city.

Strike one for the home team.

At least they weren't aluminum bats.

Flushing, New York, 1993. Another summer of discontent in the Big Apple, with the New York Mets, that is.

Banner Day at Shea Stadium. Create a sign on a bed sheet demonstrating support for the Mets, then join the pre-game parade on the field.

But how to exhibit an affinity with the lowly Mets, a team filled with high-priced talent performing at bargain-basement levels? An organization whose off-field activities made tabloid headlines, while the on-field escapades made only the funny pages. A squad of non-achievers, resting in last place, trailing even the expansion Florida club.

A Season with Bob the Beerman

The best banners directed toward the worst team? "We Bought Season Seats; Why Are You Here?", "Catch the Marlins", and "Once Again, We Just Made This To Walk On The Field. P.S. Bring Back Wally Backman."

The banner censors, sporting blue and orange Mets blazers, evidently removed the more disparaging signs before the procession began.

And now for some promotional days we'd like to see.

Astroturf Day. Bring a chunk of real grass to the ballpark, and get a section of the artificial turf from one of the sterile, geometrically-perfect, multi-use stadiums built in the early 1970's. The home team's ground crew will then use the live sod to replace the slices of carpet distributed to the fans. Eventually, all artificial surfaces will be replaced with the same weed-infested, dandelion-covered grass that grows in your front yard. Baseball, when the grass was real.

Coffee Mug Night. Twenty-two ounce, thermal-insulated, polyurethane-sealed, with the team logo. Each paying fan receives one. Great for those cold April, May, and September nights at the ballpark, when only the howling wind keeps you company. Free refills of stadium java whenever the air temperature drops below 47. Also, to keep you awake and alert, complimentary cups whenever the home team is being clobbered by more than nine runs after the second inning.

Soccer Night. With proof of admission to a baseball game, receive twelve free tickets to the nearest professional soccer game. Plus round trip transportation, a pre-game buffet, and a post-game "Meet the Kickball Team" party. And be added to the soccer team's mailing list.

Photo Day. Star players are never included in the picture collection. They don't allow distribution of their likeliness free of charge. So, a switch from the time-honored tradition of receiving autographed eight-by-ten glossies of the home team's biggest stiffs. The fan would give a color photo of himself to any player on the team. And he could include a personalized message on the picture to the player.

The possibilities are endless.

On one photo, "Dear Feeble-hitting Shortstop, My four-year

old uses more force swatting flies than you do swatting pitches. Try a whiffle ball bat." Or on another, "Dear Biscuit Head, You play the outfield with the grace of a heifer in a manure-covered pasture. Hope you fall in."

Tattoo Night. A sure-fire winner to attract a crowd type that doesn't regularly attend baseball games. These people spend most of their time on the road, on a Harley, or in a pick-up truck. The truck's color is bondo, and it has curtains and an eight-track tape deck. An ideal promotion for a niche market.

Ticket Holder Day. A clear plastic carrying case with a zip-lock top and a chain to hang it around the neck. Place into it all the really important items the fan uses at the ballpark, like the ticket, driver's license, and money. These usually are crammed into wallets, pockets, or purses, forcing the individual to rummage through his personal belongings to locate them.

And these items are used so, so often.

Returning to your seat? Into the pocket to get the ticket to show the usher. Want a beer? Into the wallet and pull the ID for proof of age. Buying a hot dog? Into the purse and dig for a ten-dollar bill.

With the clear plastic ticket holder, the fan has easy access to all this, just hanging from his neck. The stadium personnel view the ticket or driver's license through the plastic pouch. No hassle, no hunting.

Whoopee Cushion Night. A classic prank gift for more than a century. More fun than a barrel of monkeys! Was it live, or was it Memorex? Keep the lady next to you guessing all evening. Fans, no more being accused of sitting on your hands. Now you can replicate strange bodily noises without the use of hands! Applause is out. "Breaking wind" sounds are in.

And so are "Freebies, Giveaways, and Promotions."

REST ROOMS

Haven't they suffered enough?
      Beano Cook, ESPN sports commentator

What's man's greatest uncontrollable desire? A chocolate truffle after a fine dining experience? The lust for the scantily clad person strolling down a Caribbean beach? Waxing a brand new car for the fourth time in the four months owned?

All satisfy some primeval need. But are any the ultimate urge??

Nah.

Man's most irrepressible need is a rest room when the bases are loaded with two out, a full count on the batter, and YOUR team down by two runs in its last at-bat.

Now the dilemma. Should you leave YOUR seat and make the mad dash to the latrine? Or do you pray the dam doesn't break?

And it's always YOUR problem. No one else's. It's YOUR bladder about to blow, no other's.

YOUR decision.

Consider, at the ballpark or the theater, travel time to the toilet is an issue. It's beat the clock. Thirty-three seconds to climb over the fourteen people seated between you and the aisle. Provided no one is a double-seat filler. If a jumbo Frank eating a jumbo frank is in the row, add thirty seconds.

Reaching the aisle, it's eighteen seconds up to the concourse tunnel.

Ever notice whenever there's an impending bladder break, the shortest route to the relief point is always uphill, against the wind, in a driving snowstorm?? And the Partridge Family, Snow White and the Seven Dwarfs, and the Vienna Boys Choir are all returning to their seats which just happen to be in YOUR aisle. And the only vendor still working at this juncture of the game just happens to be in YOUR section.

Playing fullback up the middle, you hit the concourse in stride with the quickening contractions in YOUR mid-section. The facilities are within eye shot. Only two concession stands to pass, and it's home free.

But wait!

Interference ahead!

The bus transporting the Greater Metropolitan Organization in Support of any Youth Cause departs in five minutes. One zillion little people with exactly one chaperone are fleeing the bleachers and swarming the concourse.

Exhibiting the moves of a high school junior varsity second-team wingback you once were, you stumble, bumble, and fumble YOUR way through the toughest defense in years. Pay dirt is near. You're about to crack the plane of the end zone standing.

Crunch!

The door was slammed in YOUR face. Actually, it never budged. A handwritten sign taped to the latrine door contained a dreaded Dear John letter. OUT OF ORDER!

Forty-three seconds across the concourse for this. No leaks from the dam at least. But you still manage to get a tile streamer stuck to the bottom of your shoe.

Yanking the fourteen-foot long piece of toilet paper from your foot, it's quickly back the other way.

With YOUR bladder bloated to the size of a pregnant water buffalo, you ramble towards the promised land as gracefully as that same buffalo. Pushing old ladies aside and throwing women and children to the ground, in a matter of a New York minute, you find a functioning facility. You've made it to the beer return just as the barley river was about to foam over its banks. After the longest two minutes and thirty-four seconds, it's relief at last!

Not so fast! Once inside the promised land, you discover the urinals resemble Michelangelo's workshop on a bad day. Broken pottery everywhere.

That's ok. The dashing, dancing, prancing, and pushing to urgently find a relieving room has jarred the insides. It's time to let loose number two, too.

Just need to pick the right door. That means it must be time to play *Let's Make a Deal*.

Behind door number one, we have a newspaper, but no toilet paper.

Behind door number two, we have toilet paper, but also the great flood.

And behind door number three, it's a hand-crafted porcelain bowl filled with a special treat just for you.

Suddenly, YOUR urge disappears.

Kind of surprising how quickly Mother Nature can be quelled, isn't it??

A View from the Stands

HIGH-PRESSURE SALES PITCHES

I came into this game sane, and I want to leave it sane."
Don Baylor, Colorado Rockie manager

Ever fall for a smooth-talking salesman's spiel? Buying things which weren't needed because couldn't say no? Has the Home Shopping Network been pre-programmed into the VCR so as not to miss any bargains when away from home?

Ballpark vendors love these people. No need to waste a breath. No fast-talking sales speech. Guaranteed commission. Never a "no, thanks."

How do you respond to innovative, high-pressured sales tactics?? Here are actual fans' answers to some of the most creative sales lines used by vendors. And remember, these are actual responses by you, the reader of this book, while sitting in the stadium's stands.

Vendor's pitch: Get your delicious frozen yogurt here!
Fan's response: Yogurt, yuck.
Vendor's comeback: What's the matter, afraid of a little culture?

Vendor's pitch: One stop shopping here! Peanuts! Crackerjack! Red Ropes! Beer, heeeere! I'm a walking smorgasbord!!
Fan's response: Come back when you have the blue light special on.
Vendor's comeback: Sorry, no K-Mart prices here. Ballpark prices only.

A Season with Bob the Beerman

Vendor's pitch: Who needs peanuts to wash down that beer?
Fan's response: Don't you mean the other way around?
Vendor's comeback: Not the way I sell 'em!

Vendor's pitch: No lines, no wait! No need to get out of your seats! This Beerman delivers! I'm faster than Domino's!
Fan's response: OK, I'll have a pizza.
Vendor's comeback: I'm a Budman, not a pizza-face.

Vendor's pitch: I just sold Elvis a beer! Who's next?
Fan's response: You've been reading too much of the National Enquirer.
Vendor's comeback: It's only because my subscription to *MAD* magazine expired.

Vendor's pitch: House special tonight, folks! Cold night, warm beer! Spike that coffee with a beer!
Fan's response: How warm is it?
Vendor's comeback: Hot enough to de-fog the frost from your eyeglasses.

Vendor's pitch: Buy a beer from me, or I'll serenade you with the theme song from *The Brady Bunch*!
Fan's response: (No words, just a mass look of panic on everyone's faces. And everyone buys a beer).
Vendor's comeback: Thanks, folks, but I really don't know the words.

Vendor's pitch: Beer left over from the Pope's visit! How many of you worship beer? Who needs one?
Fan's response: Is it made from Holy Water?
Vendor's comeback: No, but I'm blessed daily by fans who thank me for bringing beer.

Vendor's pitch: Cold beer! Cold nuts! Cold licorice! Who needs a cold one!?
Fan's response: One cold one, please.
Vendor's comeback: Which cold one, sir?

A View from the Stands

Vendor's pitch: I got beer! I got 'nuts! I got 'Jacks! I got bad English. Buy my beer, send me to school!
Fan's response: One of each. I'll help send you to Harvard.
Vendor's comeback: I already did my undergrad work there.

Vendor's pitch: Crime fighter by day, Beerman by night! Who needs a cold one?
Fan's response: Which crime fighter are you?
Vendor's comeback: What crime did you commit?

Vendor's pitch: Buy a beer! Find the lucky cup! Win a brand, new Buick Riviera!
Fan's response: You've been watching too much of *The Price is Right*.
Vendor's comeback: But this may just be your *Wheel of Fortune*, Vanna included.

Vendor's pitch: Folks, this jumbo CrackerJack box just may contain the lucky Rolex watch! Who needs one?
Fan's response: Do you have a smaller box with a Timex in it?
Vendor's comeback: No, but tomorrow morning just add milk to the jumbo leftovers and you'll have breakfast cereal.

Vendor's pitch: I've just been informed by management that Madonna will be performing the national anthem tomorrow. Buy a beer to welcome her!
Fan's response: Don't think she knows the words. Then, again, she doesn't really need to know the words.
Vendor's comeback: The key word is that she's going to "perform" the national anthem.

Vendor's pitch: Fresh case of cold beer, here! Right from the cooler! My beer's so cold it still has ice on it!
Fan's response: If it's not cold enough, will I get my money back?
Vendor's comeback: If it doesn't pass the temperature test, the next beerman you see will gladly refund your money.

A Season with Bob the Beerman

Vendor's pitch: Free beer, folks! For the entire section! Choose one person to answer this question! How do you spell "Bob" backwards?
Fan's response: I'll represent the section. "Bob" spelled backwards is "b"-"o"-"b".
Vendor's comeback: Buzzzz! Nice try, but an incorrect answer. "Bob" spelled backwards is "b"- "o"-"capital "B"! Fans, this person just blew it for the entire section!

Vendor's pitch: Seventh inning, folks! I turn into a pumpkin at the end of the seventh! We stop pouring the beer then. Who needs one?!
Fan's response: I'll take Cinderella and a beer.
Vendor's comeback: Sorry, she doesn't fit into the glass slipper any more. Too many beers.

Vendor's pitch: Seventh inning! Last chance folks! Last chance to see my face! Buy my beer! Shut me up! Send me home!
Fan's response: Quick, let's buy him out. We'll finally get rid of him! (Said amid wild, jubilant applause and a standing ovation.)
Vendor's comeback: I'm ubiquitous! I'm omnipresent! I'm everywhere! I'll be back in your dreams tonight, turning them into your worst nightmares!

A View from the Stands

BUSINESSPERSON'S SPECIAL

A baseball game is twice as much fun if you're seeing it on the company's time."
William Feather, from his *The Business of Life*

Business getting you down? Need something extra to close a deal? A different setting, a little entertainment? How about the American Pastime for an alternative environment? Take the client out to the ol' ball game. See some sports, feast on food, burp up beer, consummate the contract. Simple as that.

So, what does it take to do business at the ballpark? Modern technology, a flexible expense account, and good seats.

Out of town or crosstown, business is business. Write the memo, conduct the meeting, seal the sale, there is no need for a smoke-filled board room. All this is done at the stadium.

Bob the Beerman conducts all his affairs there. Clients come from miles, even states away, to do business with Bob. Corporate officers, real estate moguls, and TV lawyers also conduct activities at the old ball game. And not just with Bob.

At one sun-baked Thursday afternoon game, a leveraged buyout of a crowbar manufacturing company went down. Once the deal was done, Bob the Beerman poured the celebratory champagne, err, beer. Got a nice fat tip, and some stock options from the new CEO.

Bob the Beerman reaped the benefits from that transaction with no involvement required. But at times, Bob played an integral part in the deal.

While acting as intermediary between a flower wholesaler and

88

A Season with Bob the Beerman

ex-NBA coach and broadcaster Doug Moe, Bob the Beerman spent the first three innings of a Sunday afternoon game relaying counteroffers.

The Flower Man wanted court-side seats for a National Basketball Association game. And what better way to obtain them then from Moe, whose involvement with the NBA dates back to the early 70's and possibly beyond. Doug wouldn't admit to when he first reached the professional level.

From his location two-thirds up in the section behind home plate, the Flower Man spotted Moe below settling into a first row seat against the backstop. He waived me over, and made a proposal for my services.

"Beercan Bob, do me a favor," the Flower Man began. "I'll promise to buy all my ballpark food from you for the rest of the season. All you have to do is help me get some prime basketball tickets."

Beerman gave him a skeptical look, but before he had a chance to utter a sound, the Flower Man upped the ante.

"I'll throw in a gift certificate for Valentine's Day flowers too. See Doug Moe down there? Buy him a beer. Point out to him that it's from me. Then tell him I'll send flowers on his behalf to his wife on all the major flower-giving holidays. All this in exchange for a pair of court-side seats. And give him my card. I'll pencil the deal on the back of it. Ok?"

Once the ante was upped with the gift certificate, Bobster took the deal. After all, free flowers on Valentine's Day? How could anyone pass? Numerous women will be receiving floral arrangements. The old black book will get a work out. Bob's bound to get one or two dates from this set-up. And can't forget mom, grandma - both of them, his six sisters, and his female office staff at Beerman Industries. But all that is another chapter.

So the Bobarama bounded down the aisle and went to work.

"Excuse me, sir," Bob said, pretending not to know it was with Doug Moe he was talking. "That gentleman standing and waving about twenty rows up the aisle bought you this beer."

Moe turned toward the Flower Man and raised his beer glass in recognition.

"Nice guy," Moe began. "But for some reason, people like buying me beer. Must be my stylish wardrobe."

A View from the Stands

"Actually, I'm not quite sure that's it," Beerman said. "You see, that fellow is a florist, and he's offered to send your wife flowers on your behalf on all the relevant holidays and anniversaries. Free of charge."

Moe took a swig from his beer as he pondered my words.

"He even put it in writing," Bob added. "Here's his business card with the offer penned on the backside. All he wants are a couple of tickets to a hoops game."

The ex-NBA coach studied the card, then turned toward the Flower Man and gave the thumbs up sign.

"I get more complimentary things than I know what to do with. And that includes basketball tickets. But don't tell him I told you that," said Moe. "Besides, this flower arrangement will come in handy. Tell him I'll phone him later to confirm."

With that, the BobMeister hiked up the aisle to relay the message to the Flower Man.

"Looks like you got yourself a deal," Bob said. "He'll give you a buzz about the logistics. And I'll send you a list of women for my end of the bargain."

It was only August, but Valentine's Day couldn't come soon enough.

Unfortunately, all of Bob the Beerman's ballpark dealings didn't involve love and harmony.

You see, at another midweek businessperson's special, Beercan Bob witnessed a messy custody battle. The lawyer to the first party, Attorney FirstSideOfTheLaw, sat immediately behind the first base dugout. This prime spot was the season ticket location of his client, Mr. Season Seats.

Attorney F. worked his cellular phone to the brink of battery extinction.

"We'll get another restraining order!" barked F. into the cordless. "She'll never get one, let alone both! Hold on, I'll check."

Dropping the phone from his lips, F. said to his client, "She'll contribute $500 a month for each one. What do you think?"

"Up it to $900 and use of the Aspen home every other weekend during ski season," Mr. Season Seats answered, as he punched some numbers into his pocket computer. "But the Laguna Beach house is off limits."

A Season with Bob the Beerman

F. passed this counteroffer along via the cellular to the opposing lawyer, Mr. SecondSideOfTheLaw. After what seemed like an indeterminable pause, F. presented a counter-counteroffer to Season Seats.

"She accepts, but only if she gets custody of both every other weekend," F. said to Mr. Seats. "You can have both of them the rest of the time."

"Ok. Knowing my ex, I won't get anything better than this," conceded Seats. "I agree. Let's get it in writing."

Attorney F. clicked off the phone's mute button and gave the approval to Attorney S.

"The fax is on its way outlining everything," F. said. "Just sign it and send it back."

Out of F.'s pocket came a cellular fax machine. He inserted the hand-drawn agreement into the intake feed and punched in the phone number. Soon, the letter was on it's way to S.

It was only a matter of seconds before the signed agreement returned from S. via the fax. That was followed by a ring of F.'s cordless.

"Got it," said F. "It looks good. Nice doing business with you again S. Are you working on the Dr. Kevorkian case still? Oh? That's good to hear. See you at the country club Saturday for our 9:00 a.m. tee-off. Don't work too hard the rest of the afternoon.

"What? You're where?" an incredulous F. inquired. "You're at the ballpark? I'm at the ballpark too!"

With that, Attorney F. clicked off the cellular, arose from Mr. Season Seats prime first row location, turned, and waved to Attorney S., who was sitting in the upper deck with the ex-Mrs. Season Seats.

"I took care of your case pretty well, eh, Season?" F. boasted to Mr. Seats. "She only gets custody of the season tickets every second weekend. The way the home schedule falls, she'll only see about fifteen games."

"Hey, beerman!" F. yelled to Bob. "Two cold ones to toast another case won."

Turning back to Mr. Seats, F. asked, "Say, what do you do with the kids when you're here at the ballpark?"

A View from the Stands

FINANCIAL MARKETS AND BALLPLAYERS

The baseball mania has run its course. It has no future as a professional endeavor.
   The Cincinnati *Gazette*, 1879

“ The Dow Industrials' Average was up seven and one-half points today. Gainers outpaced losers, two to one, as twenty-seven professional baseball players took themselves public with a stock offering. Trading under Baseball Inc., of America, the combined net worth of this group is estimated to be $810 million.”

An actual report heard on the radio? Not today, but possibly in the very near future.

And it wouldn't be found on the sports' segments of the news. Look under the business section.

Instead of checking the box scores to see how Mighty Casey did in last night's game, people are scanning the stock quotes to find at what price their favorite players are trading.

"Hey, Bonds went ex-dividend yesterday, his stock price dropped one and three-fourths," one commuter said to another, as he scanned the *Wall Street Journal* on the 8:15 train into the city. "If it falls another two points, it could jeopardize his balance sheet."

"Let's see. A drop of one and three-fourths? That means his batting average should drop about fifteen to twenty points," remarked the second commuter, a bond trader for Salomon Brothers. "And that could cause him to lose the MVP award and its four-million-dollar bonus."

A Season with Bob the Beerman

"That would cause a downward spiral effect on his stock price. Guess that means he'll want to renegotiate his contract with the team ASAP to hedge against that," added the first, an international investor. "It's only the third time this season he's renegotiated. Count on him to sit out tonight's game until his team's owners ante up on his latest demands."

"If he's out tonight, does that increase the unemployment rate?" asked the second. "Does that mean recessionary times are coming?"

"Nah, he's only one individual," the first answered. "But remember the one year when forty-five one-plus-million-dollar-a-year players went unsigned? That had a negative statistical impact on the jobless rate. Any time you have over seven percent out of work in a given industry, you know things are rough."

"And think of the GNP effect of not having all those millions of dollars in circulation," added the second. "The money supply is just drying up."

"That's what the baseball owners have been crying for years," chipped in the first. "And now the players are also complaining that the money supply from the owners is dwindling. And the television networks gripe they don't have the cash stream coming from advertisers any more for sports broadcasting. So they won't pay the big money for the rights to telecast ball games."

"Everyone's groaning about the shrinking money supply, but it's us, the fan, who gets stuck footing the bill for all the greedy, egotistical parties involved," lamented the second. "Market economics just aren't taking place in the professional sports business."

"The interest rate markets will take a beating because of this," the first added. "In five to seven years, the long term interest rates will plummet. Who will want to go to games or watch them on TV? Ten years from now, people just won't be interested in professional sports any more."

Turning to the sports section of *The Times* and scanning its headlines, the second blurted, "Hey, did you see Mr. October, Reggie Jackson, is coming out of retirement? He just signed a mega-deal with the Tokyo Dragons of the Japanese League for an reported eight-point-six-billion yen over two years!"

A View from the Stands

"That's old news. I saw it on the foreign currency market pages of the business section," the first replied. "There goes the value of the dollar."

The train pulled into it's final stop in the city and the doors swung open. As the two gathered their belongings and departed, the international investor said to his bond trader friend, "Don't forget the charity softball game in the park tonight. And everyone's kicking in a buck for the keg of beer."

HEALTH-CONSCIOUS APPROACH TO BASEBALL

I was X-rayed so often I glowed in the dark.
    Billy Grabarkewitz, former utility infielder

Working too hard? Long hours in the office leading to anxiety attacks? Company's coffee burning a hole in the styrofoam cup, not to mention the stomach? Tired of lunch from the aluminum-sided Chuck Wagon canteen?

Then take-in a baseball game, at an outdoor park, bathed in the green and blue of freshly cut grass against a cloudless sky. And shopping carefully, you can dine on fat-free, highly-nutritious, ballpark cuisine in a stress-free environment.

After a day or two at the old ball yard, you'll be fit for life. Or until the boss tells you tomorrow's report was due on his desk yesterday.

So, how will a baseball game make you healthier, you wonder?

Glad you asked.

To start, time spent at a ball game is time away from work. The less time spent slaving away for the company, the healthier you are. Both emotionally and physically.

Catching a ball game means catching a sanity break from job pressures. Where would you rather be, under the fluorescent glow from the desk lamp? Or under a sun-splashed sky in an open-air arena? Just the thought of being at an outdoor ballpark makes you feel more well-adjusted, right?

No need to wear the work uniform there, either. Rip off the tie

A View from the Stands

and jacket, loosen up the collar, hop out of those coveralls.

Put on a pair of bermuda shorts, tennis shoes, and a golf shirt. Let the fresh air blow across your bare skin. You'll be much more comfortable doing the ball yard exercises too.

"A work-out at the stadium??" you ask.

"Sure, you'll see," I answer. "And how much exercise do you get at work??"

Walk to the water cooler. Walk past the water cooler to the rest room. Walk back to your work space.

At that rate, your resting heart rate is just above deceased.

The only time the old blood pumper gets a work-out is when you participate in the fax toss. This happens when you try to transmit to a counterpart across the country a project which took six months to produce. Only, the fax machine decides it's hungry and devours your paperwork. The cover sheet is the only remnant. You then try to hurl the machine out the window to your counterpart's location.

You figure if the fax machine lands at the destination, it may just regurgitate the fax.

A much more active lifestyle exists at the ballpark.

Parking the car in a different time zone from the stadium, you have a two-mile hike to the game. Once inside the gates, awaiting is a two-mile vertical hike to your seats.

That's four miles one way. No way you could get that much exercise in a month at the sweatshop, I mean place of employment.

Don't you feel much more cardiovascularly fit now that you've reached your seat? And you haven't started diving for foul balls yet.

Now, there's the need to replenish the lost nutrients after a strenuous work-out.

On the job, it means a bologna sandwich on white bread wrapped in plastic wrap, with a pair of shriveled dill pickle spears on the side. Can't you feel the arteries hardening? Can't you feel the stale bread sticking to the roof of your mouth?

No need to worry about this at the ballpark. Dietary dining delights here.

Fresh garden salad to start, but stay away from the creamy

dressings. Fulfills the roughage requirement. It will help purge your system of Chuck Wagon's wonder food - wonder what the growth of the month is on this food?

Next, go with the steamed veggie hot dog. Add relish, onions, and black bean chili. That covers the protein, fruits and vegetables, and breads and grains groups. High in vitamins, minerals and fiber, it's a perfect entree.

And besides, steaming is one of the best ways to preserve nutrients when cooking food. Always go with steamed ballpark food. Stay away from the thermonuclear-prepared food. Radiation sickness has been reported in people consuming microwaved food. Not to mention microwaving jams the walkman's radio reception of the ball game.

Desert from the canteen? Fourteen-day-old shoo fly pie, only it looks like the flies forgot to shoo. Can you identify the insect by the sound of the crunch when biting into a piece of the pie?

At the game, the choice is frozen yogurt. Cool, refreshing, and low fat, a perfect topping to an almost vegetarian meal.

The beverage of choice from Chuck's in the work place? Past-dated chocolate milk in a soggy, over-saturated cardboard carton.

But have a light beer in the stands. You're allowed one indulgence. Taste great, less filling. It covers the carbohydrate, protein, and liquid groups. Need those fluids to wash all of Chuck Wagon's impurities from your system.

Fresh air, normal clothes, light, healthy cuisine, a ball game. Don't you feel cleansed and refreshed? Ready to take on the world tomorrow in the office, right?

OK, see you back out at the ballpark again tomorrow.

A View from the Stands

RADIO DAZE

The announcer says, 'Will the lady who lost her nine children at the ballpark please pick them up immediately. They are beating the Cubs, 10-0, in the seventh.'
Tom Dreesen, 1981, quoted in *The Cubbies* by Bob Chieger

The men behind the microphone. Short men, fat men. Men with bulbous noses straining under the weight of Coke-bottle eyeglasses. Some speak Brooklynese, others have a drawl as thick as the air on a late summer Southern night. Many have their own fractured language. A few emit poetic prose. These faceless voices are your eyes and ears for the action on the ball field.

Some learned the craft from the Old School, others from the New. Some are from No School. And the rest are from the Baseball School.

Each gives us the story in his signature way. Some reporting is served with style and grace. Other's are delivered with the attitude of a subway commuter during rush hour.

At times, it's difficult to digest. The dressing may be too spicey or too sweet. Each flavor is unique. The presentation may differ, but in the end, you're left with a familiar taste. They all give the final score.

The Old School sportscasters cultivated their trade when the grass was real. Games were played at ball fields named Wrigley and ballparks christened Fenway. The Baseball God's chose Mother Sun to enlighten its stage. The characters were costumed in real flannels and black spit-shined spikes, with each inning a new act in a Shakespearean drama.

The seasoned sportscaster was the Greek orator. His words told of the daily conflicts and crises between the two combatants. As the tide changed and the winds blew, the announcer from the Classical years painted a picture that could be hung along side the Masters.

Through his descriptions from a thousand miles away, you could "see" the mustard-stained hot dog wrapper dancing the fox trot across the blades of freshly trimmed grass as it attempted to elude the clutches of the infield dust devil.

Those trained under the Old School could compose a Neo-classic masterpiece with only the three basic colors. The New School students learned to create with a sixty-four-pack of Crayola.

Educated with advanced college degrees from places like Harvard, the New Schoolers possess an unparalleled vocabulary and a broad spectrum of conversational knowledge.

These announcers are the Modernists of the profession. Not only can they report a pitcher's ERA, but they are also able to derive it mathematically. And they know the chemical composition of both pine tar and the rosin bag.

Though not as skilled at creating the picture as the classical sportscasters, the New Schoolers' artwork has all the basic parts in the proper order. They'll also quote you a price for their services, as well as the salary scale for the home team's players.

Well spoken, with vocal ranges a choir director would love, these New Schoolers are behind a microphone and not in front of the television camera because their voices are better groomed than the rest of the body. They can operate all the latest electronic technological gadgets except the blow dryer and the electric razor. Despite names more suited to television, their poor camera presence leaves them behind the microphone.

But if Scooter and Harry are names attached to the Old Schoolers, and Ryan and Gordon belong to the New School graduates, then Homer Pumpkinhead and Billy Joe Earwax define the No Schoolers. Their skills developed by doing the calls on the minor league circuit, for teams like the Thunder Bay WhiskeyJacks and the Charleston RiverDogs.

Through hard work, some eventually make it to the big

A View from the Stands

leagues. Unfortunately, their dialects never advanced past the Single A level.

Each school has its own idioms and colloquialisms.

The Old Schoolers have "Holy Cow!", "It's Outta Here!", and "That's all folks!". The New Schoolers have "Yes!", "Do you believe in Miracles?", and "I'm going to Walt Disney World!".

The No Schoolers have "Might just see some hiiitin' and run action happenin' heere," and "Dat ball went outta heere fasta dan a mo-skee-toe in heete!"

Local color on big league games by polyester-wearing, truck-camper driving, alligator-wrasslin' announcers tests the FCC decency clause. Luckily, most don't make it past broadcasting for the Double A Chattanooga Chooos. Abstract defines the way they present their trade.

Then there are those from the Ballplayer School. These out of shape ex-jocks are walking advertisements for Rogaine, ThighMaster, and the Bullworker. In desperate need of money after their baseball careers are complete, they turn to broadcasting.

With all the handiwork of a fourth grade finger painter, their portrayals of the action are often buried in garbled radio signal reception. It's not because of sun spot activity or radar jamming devices. It's due to the ex-players broadcasting while packing a wad of tobacco between their cheek and gum. The static is actually the player attempting to pontificate without spitting, slobbering, or dribbling chew all over the microphone.

Occasionally, these members from the Ballplayer School have great insight and anecdotes to what's transpiring on the field. Only problem is deciphering the words from the other strange sounds ex-ballplayers emit. If able to decode that, you can just hope the story doesn't have such an inside meaning that the only people to comprehend it are other baseballers. If that's the case, dead air is a better alternative.

Just pray that you can understand the final score.

BASEBALL STRATEGY

Any time you think you have the game conquered, the game will turn around and punch you right in the nose."
    Mike Schmidt, former Phillie third baseman and soon-to-be Hall of Famer

A recent CNN / USA TODAY poll revealed startling facts about the average fan's knowledge of baseball.

Fifty-five percent had no clue as to the difference between a passed ball and a wild pitch.

Twenty percent couldn't determine why the manager played the percentages and brought in a left-handed relief pitcher to face a left-handed batter.

Twelve percent thought a squeeze play was something immoral.

Eight percent thought ballplayers scratching and adjusting themselves was grotesque.

And five percent responded that they had no response to their interest in the level of baseball understanding.

At least the last five took time to try to comprehend the survey questioning their comprehension of baseball.

Some additional findings:

Q: *Should pitchers be allowed to throw the spitball?*

Sixty percent said only if chewing tobacco wasn't used.

Thirty percent answered only if the pitchers brushed their teeth that morning.

Ten percent replied only with their mother's approval.

Q: *When is the best time to sacrifice?*

Fifty-five percent answered when there's men on base.

A View from the Stands

Thirty-five percent said when you blow off your wife's homemade lasagna dinner to attend the Opening Day game.

Ten percent suggested any time you could get out of visiting your in-laws.

Q: *When is a hit and run most successful?*

The majority answered when the police are on break at the local donut shop.

A handful suggested when a big, slow, fat guy is in the on-deck circle.

Q: *Is the black border around home plate part of the strike zone?*

Forty percent answered when it wasn't covered by dirt.

Thirty-five percent suggested it didn't make a difference. Umpires are basically blind anyway.

And fifteen percent were non-union respondents. They didn't understand the theory behind the strike zone.

Q: *Why do managers remove starting pitchers after a pre-determined pitch count?*

A whopping seventy-two percent had no idea.

Fourteen percent said it had to do with a performance clause negotiated into the player's contract.

Ten percent thought it was because the manager had money riding on the game and he had to keep it close.

Four percent wanted to know if their bosses could replace them when they started getting tired at about three o'clock each afternoon.

Q: *How late in the game should a manager replace his all-hit, no-field third baseman with a weak-hitting defensive specialist?*

Sixty percent felt in the eight inning and with a three-run-or-less lead was the appropriate time.

Twenty-five percent answered never. The late game defensive replacement is prone to choking and making a two-run throwing error in crucial situations.

Fifteen percent thought the team mascot could be brought in, because the odds of a ball being hit to that position at that juncture were too small.

Q: *When is the best time to issue an intentional walk?*

Fifty percent replied never, that it's the chicken's way out.

A Season with Bob the Beerman

The players are getting paid big bucks, so they should go down fighting.

Twenty-five percent said when a televised game is moving too quickly for the network. Intentional walks make the game longer, allowing more commercials to be aired.

Fifteen percent didn't realize it was an intentional walk. They thought it was just a case of Wild-Thing-itis.

Ten percent thought it was when the pitcher had money riding on the game in the opposite direction of his manager and needed a blow-out to win the bet.

If the legendary baseball strategist Casey Stengel was alive today, what would his reaction be to this poll?

"Polls? I love Poles? Love the food. The kielbasa, pierogies, and especially the Polish sausages!"

A View from the Stands

No Drinking and Driving

I have found most baseball players to be afflicted with tobacco-chewing minds.
  Howard Cosell, former ABC announcer

What if auto makers, beer companies, and the tobacco industry weren't sponsors of major league baseball?? How would the game be different?

There would be no commercials of ex-jocks swigging beer with bikini-clad women. That's one less occupational field for ex-ballplayers. And it's one less way hormonally imbalanced men have to entertain themselves.

There would be no Clydesdale-drawn wagon, no Rocky Mountain landscapes, no "Taste Great, Less Filling."

There would be an awful lot of dead air to fill.

There would be no power car advertisements. No slinky long-haired blonds in flowing gowns making love to a sleek sports car. No road-handling, wheels-squealing, aerodynamic driving action.

There would be an awful lot of blank ad pages in newspapers and magazines.

There would be no Marlboro man, no Bull Durham. There would be no camera shots of players with bloated cheeks dribbling brown spit down their chins. No more pictures of ballplayers sneaking drags on a butt in a dark corner of the dugout.

There would be an awful lot of empty billboards around the stadium.

If the car manufacturers stopped sponsorship, there would be no more "Baseball, hot dogs, apple pie, and Chevrolet."

If breweries ceased its sports advertising program, there

would be no more "Bud Bowl."

If tobacco companies ended its commercial campaign targeted at the athletic audience (definitely a paradox), there would be no more Joe Cool the Camel.

So how would the game change?

The air at the ballpark would be cleaner. Gone would be the cigarette smoke, automobile exhaust, and beer belches. Less carbon monoxide and airborne pollutants means the grass would be greener. And so would the Astroturf - no cigarette burns or tobacco stains.

The games would be quicker. Hitters would no longer step out of the batter's box between pitches to reload their mouth with a wad of chew. And the umpire would no longer need to wait for commercial clearance from a television producer before he could order "Batter-up!" to start each half inning.

Kids would actually be able to stay up to watch the conclusion of a World Series game if there was no beer, auto, and tobacco commercials.

Stadiums would no longer be such a drab place, once the billboards were removed. These signs could be replaced by the works of local artists, like those that produce masterpieces on building facades and on the undersides of bridges. This modern art would sure bring a symmetrical, cookie cutter stadium to life.

Come to think of it, I'd be willing to bring back beer, tobacco, and car billboards that adorned old ball yards if it meant getting rid of those round, generic, multi-purpose stadiums. Call it my field of dreams.

A View from the Stands

PRESS CONFERENCE LANGUAGE

I can remember a reporter asking for a quote, and I didn't know what a quote was. I thought it was some kind of a soft drink.
    Joe DiMaggio, the Yankee Clipper and Hall of Fame member

The average sports fan understands the play on the field. A ball hit over the fence - in fair territory, of course - is a home run. The home team loses by fourteen, it's a rout - for both baseball and football. The pitcher walks the bases loaded, then walks in the winning run - he should be executed on the spot.

The action on the diamond is easy to comprehend. After all, it's right there in front of your eyes, and seeing is believing. Just ask the media types who cover the game. The players, coaches, and managers tell it like it is in post-game interviews. Their quotes explain what happened during the contest. Never a doubt why the home team didn't pinch-hit for Smitty. You can understand why Hans Ofstone struck out four times and had three errors. It's as simple as what the players said to the television and newspaper reporters.

It would be plainly clear if ballplayers spoke in a tongue that was common to the other 4.3 billion people on this planet. Between ball yard jargon, small town accents, and cynicism of the press, what spews from a ballplayer's lips isn't what's actually meant.

Here are translations of baseball quotes to their true meanings.

A Season with Bob the Beerman

Player says: We were just a little bit flat today.
Interpretation: We've given up on the season. We're forty-one and one-half games out of first, and all we want to do is end this debacle of a season and get out to the golf courses.

Player says: The pitch was in my sweet spot. I got great lumber on it, and the rest was history.
Interpretation: The pitcher has no velocity and no movement on the ball any more. He grooved it right down the center of the plate, and even though I had my eyes closed, I was lucky enough to make contact and hit it out of this match box stadium.

Player says: The umpire's a fat blindman who was out of position to make the call. Everyone in the stadium could see I was safe. The $&%# ump has a personnel vendetta against me.
Interpretation: I ignored the stop sign from my third base coach because if I scored it would have given me 100 runs for the season and a $200,000 incentive bonus in my contract would have kicked in. I probably never should have tried to score from second on the slow roller up the middle. I screwed up and cost us the game. But I'm not the first person on this team to make a mistake and blow a win.

Player says: I threw one terrible pitch to the wrong hitter. It could happen to anybody.
Interpretation: All my pitches are bad. Some are just worse than others. My arm's dead, but our team has no one else on the pitching staff that's even half as good as me. What are they going to do, fire me?

Player says: The ball was just out of my reach.
Interpretation: If I hadn't put on thirty-five pounds in the last year, I may have been able to get to the ball. But now I have a hard time bending over to field those grounders. Besides, if I dove for it, I could have soiled my uniform, costing me money in endorsements.

A View from the Stands

Player says: I lost it in the sun.
Interpretation: I was too busy checking out the brunette in the second row bulging out of her bikini top.

Player says: That pitcher is going to win the Cy Young Award with stuff like that.
Interpretation: I couldn't hit this guy if he was tossing beach balls and I had an over-sized tennis racquet for a bat.

Player says: I've got a pulled muscle in my leg. I think I overtrained.
Interpretation: I strained a thigh muscle putting on my pants because I let myself get too far out of shape.

Manager says: We're a young, aggressive team, with our future ahead of us.
Interpretation: If we finish higher than last place, we'll be lucky. Our team is slightly more experienced than a high school varsity squad. And we can't hit, field, or throw strikes, so we'll be hustling all over the field chasing down wild pitches and overthrown balls.

Manager says: It was an opportune time to make the switch.
Interpretation: The manager received a phone call in the dugout from the owner instructing him to make the pitching change.

Manager says: On paper, we match up with any team.
Interpretation: On the field, we'll get our behinds handed to us.

Manager says: This is as close as I've been to any of my teams.
Interpretation: I've had to bail half the guys out of jail at one time or another. About a quarter of my ballplayers are so young I've had to change their diapers. And to the rest I've had to play counselor.

Manager says: We need to work on our fundamentals.
Interpretation: Our players have no idea what to do with the batted baseball once they actually catch it.

Manager says: Just one or two more key hits, and the outcome would have been different.
Interpretation: We would have lost by two touchdowns instead of three. That's not too bad, considering our guys don't know how to hold the bat, let alone swing it and make contact with the ball.

Manager says: Experience is on our side.
Interpretation: The locker room reeks of Ben-Gay and wrinkle remover. We have a team of old geezers, has-beens, never-has-beens, and washed-up utility players. We need every ointment, liniment, and potential fountain of youth to keep the blood flowing and bodies from stiffening. These guys should be on the Seniors' Professional Golf tour.

Manager says: We weren't exactly ripping the balls off the covers.
Interpretation: We weren't exactly ripping the covers off the balls.

And the fan thinks, "This was just starting to make sense to me."

A View from the Stands

LET'S PLAY TWO

The only reason I'm coming out here tomorrow is the schedule says I have to.
    Sparky Anderson, Detroit Tiger manager

Every real baseball fan should attend one doubleheader before moving on to the great bleacher section in the sky. Just kick back, catch some rays and fresh air, have a beer and a dog or two. It's two games for the price of one. If the home team loses the first, there's the opportunity for revenge in the second.

Of course, the fan can come and go as he pleases. He can arrive halfway through the first game, catch its conclusion, then split midway through the second contest if it's a rout.

For us beer men, there is no such luxury. We're working for the duration. And we don't get time-and-a-half for overtime. No strolling into the ballpark in the fourth inning like the casual fan. No showering and changing of uniforms between games like the players. No air-conditioned private stadium suite to escape the heat like the owners.

We just sweat, starting with the

11:30 a.m. commute to the ballpark. That's when Bob the Beerman departs from home in his John Madden land-cruising bus clone.

1:00 p.m. Check-in time for this early September twin bill. The organist is the only person to arrive earlier. He's already playing the sound track to "Frivolous Ballpark Melodies."

1:10 p.m. As we sit in the obstructed-view seats getting chewed out, err, our vending assignments, we catch glimpses of the players

A Season with Bob the Beerman

arriving in their Jaguars, Mercedes, and BMW's. We also see one vendor arriving late on his Schwinn Varsity ten-speed bike.

1:45 p.m. Roll call is complete. Time to battle the fans in the left field stands for batting practice home run balls to the organist's beat of "Cheery Baseball-Type Tunes."

2:15 p.m. Bob foregoes the jousting competition in the outfield bleachers. Early in the season, the Bobster was steamrolled by a roly-poly fourteen-year-old in pursuit of a batting practice ball. In turn, the teenager was buffaloed by a rotund forty-year-old man reliving his childhood by going Kamikaze for the ball. The middle-aged fellow recovered the batted ball. The kid received a souvenir ball from a player standing in left who witnessed the assault. Bob got some bumps and bruises. The Organist played "Another One Bites the Dust."

2:55 p.m. The managers exchange line-up cards at home plate. A fan asks Bob where he could find some plates to pour his Chinese food onto. Chinese food??

3:15 p.m. The top of the first ends with a pop out to first. And the Bobarama pops open his last full beer and ends his first case.

4:20 p.m. After five fast-paced but scoreless innings, Bob is also getting shut out. On three separate occasions, women turn down Bob's offer of complimentary beers in exchange for their phone numbers.

5:05 p.m. Seventh inning stretch time. The work day is over and the crowd finally begins to arrive en masse. Good. It's about time. Beercan Bob has discussed *War and Peace* with everyone who's been in the stands for the first six innings. He's getting tired of saying Tolstoy.

And the organist plays the traditional stretch song "Take Me Out to the Ball Game" for the sixty-seventh time this season. And for the sixty-seventh time, he misplays it. Kind of sounds normal now.

5:40 p.m. As the stadium lights flicker on, the first two runs of the game cross home. The Bobinator breathes easier. Didn't want to see extra innings in the first game of a DH. The evening could have turned into an all-nighter.

5:50 p.m. The last beer of the third case is poured as the last out of the first contest is recorded. "Twenty minutes between games," blares the public address announcer. In other words, potty break. And more bad organ music.

111

A View from the Stands

6:08 p.m. The third base coaches for each team meet at home plate to swap line-ups. Get the feeling it's going to be a long night when the managers are so tired they send their bench assistants to perform the effortless pre-game ritual?

6:12 p.m. "Play ball," cries the umpire, feigning an excited tone for this second half of the twin bill between two of the three worst teams in the league.

6:48 p.m. After twenty-three batters, fifteen hits, twelve runs, and five pitchers, the first inning finally ends. Bob sells two pitchers, err, cases of cold ones, a dozen bags of peanuts, and a load of CrackerJack in the marathon inning. That's an uninspired five cases of beer on the day.

7:10 p.m. The umpire behind the plate gets beaned with a warm-up pitch between innings. The game is delayed for eighteen minutes, as he is wheeled into the clubhouse to be X-rayed, MRIed, stethoscoped, or asked to turn his head and cough.

7:45 p.m. The third inning expires, as does Rick the SuperFan in section 103 who's been downing cold ones since the gates opened almost seven hours ago. The aroma of the passing bratwurst man revives him though. It's the smell of the bratwurst, not the vendor, that brings him back to life. We think.

8:55 p.m. The organist plays "Jump!". This creates a stir, as thirty thousand eyelids crack open.

9:30 p.m. A football score, seventeen to fourteen in the fourth quarter, err, sixth inning. Bob wipes out his ninth case of beer and begins to peddle No-Doz and muscle relaxants to those experiencing the effects of rigor mortis from sitting in the same position since early afternoon.

10:15 p.m. Top of the seventh. The Bobberooski is now selling breakfast burritos and beer.

10:25 p.m. Middle of the seventh. The organist abandons "Take Me Out" in favor of Sinatra's "My Way." Somehow, the lines "And now, the end is near," seems prophetic.

10:45 p.m. One out to go in the bottom of the seventh, last call time. No takers for beer. There is one request to make a call to a fan's wife to let her know that he really is still at the ball game.

10:54 p.m. The last out is tallied. In the seventh inning. But that's Bob's cue to cut off the cold ones and check out.

11:23 p.m. Bob turns in his empties, cashes out, and tosses his

A Season with Bob the Beerman

costume into the uniform laundry area. Before exiting the park, he takes a quick glance over his shoulder to check the inning. Still the eighth.

11:29 p.m. Bob boards his bus and immediately passes out from exhaustion. Ten hours on his feet, nine-plus miles walked - including one and a quarter vertical miles, all while hauling forty pounds of foodstuff and five pounds of loose change.

12:25 a.m. Beat Bob arrives home and does a belly flop into bed. He sleeps for forty days and nights. Or at least he thinks he did. He has to work an afternoon game tomorrow.

Editor's note: To this day, Bob does not know who won that second ball game. If you know the final score, please let Bob know the next time you see him.

A View from the Stands

YESTERDAY'S DUDS

When I was in baseball and you went into the clubhouse, you didn't see ball players with curling irons."
　　Red Barber, all-time great announcer

"Give me the basics in life, like clothes, food, and a roof over my head," said Hack Wheat, a throwback to yesteryear. "All I need are a few simple things."

"I believe in that theory," answered Trebor Zehcnod, a cosmopolitan athlete. "Except I prefer designer labels, French cuisine, and a home by Frank Lloyd Wright."

"Figured. You modern ballplayers are all the same," Wheat came back. "Making the big bucks, and everything becomes materialistic. Even your game uniforms have to be hand-sewn and form-fitting. It was never like that in my day."

"Yeah, when you played, the horsehide ball still had the animal attached. In your time, Doubleday was the inventor of baseball. In my time, he owns the Mets."

"Just goes to show you how he sold out his family's small town values of Cooperstown for the bright lights of New York City."

"That's because he got tired of wearing those baggy, dark-wool clothes of your generation. He wanted to switch to something lightweight, yet functional; colorful, yet stylish."

"It was my generation that set the tone for you modern players," interrupted Hack. "Those fancy threads you guys sport on the diamond today got it's roots from my gray flannel uniforms."

"The only thing I see similar is that we're still wearing knickers, sort of."

"You young guys even let the hemline drop on your baseball pants. It's practically to the shoe top. Pretty soon you'll be cuffing the pants."

"Hmm, not a bad idea. May just help me get another modeling gig in *GQ*."

"You know, our uniform pants had sliding pads in them to protect our backsides from brush burns. We'd slide in hard to second base to break-up a double play, and we'd put a hole right through the flannels. Get a mean-ass strawberry bruise on the butt if you didn't have those pads in."

"Never had one of those."

"That's because you modern guys never slide any more. Got too much junk in your rear pockets nowadays. A tin of tobacco, sunflower seeds, four packs of gum, batting gloves, personal address book, miscellaneous jewelry, and a take-out menu from the deli around the corner from the ballpark."

"You're exaggerating a bit. I don't chew any more."

"And at least the flannels were baggy enough to cushion the impact from our head-first dives. Sometimes it would even absorb the blood from the bruising slides."

"You guys would actually bleed when you played?"

"All the time. With the shoes we wore, you could count on getting some major league lacerations on the shins on any close play at a base. Our spit-polished black spikes looked like they weighed a ton, and they did. But all were carefully maintained. We filed our spikes to a point before every game."

"You actually sharpened your spikes?" Trebor asked in disbelief. "The union won't allow us to do anything like that today. Something about workman's comp."

"There's no need for spikes today, with all these domed stadiums and artificial grass fields. Matter of fact, you guys have rubber cleats or something like that on the bottom of your shoes, right?"

"We call it turf, or multi-purpose athletic footwear. They can be used for a variety of physical activities on diverse surfaces. They're even worn around town at social functions."

"The only reason you guys wear them in public is because you're making almost as much money from the shoe contracts as from the baseball contracts."

"That's not necessarily true! Some are quite stylish. And they match both the everyday wardrobe and the baseball uniform."

"Those double-knit, synthetic skin-tight monstrosities that look like they belong on a high-wire act in the circus? Pleease! I'll take my steamy-hot flannels any time."

"You hit it right on the head. Steamy-hot. The artificial fibers in our uniforms allow them to conform to the body, and breathe as necessary. The material actually wicks away moisture and heat from the body, but keeps water and the cold out."

"And where does the moisture and heat go?"

"Don't ask me, ask the team dry cleaner."

"At least we knew where the heat and moisture went with our uniforms. They both stayed right in them. Made our pinstipes look that much more profound."

"You mean the legendary Yankee pinstripes originated on your uniforms?"

"Sure did. And so did those striped socks and stirrups. Of course, the fans don't know what color your generation's stirrups are. They're hidden by those full-length stretch pants."

"OK, ok, lay off our fashion statement."

"You know, in addition to the pinstripes, it was my generation that first placed numbers on the jerseys. And team names and emblems too. Guess you could say that we laid the groundwork for this whole mascot and mass merchandising craze."

"Please, how can you take credit for all that? Your generation gave us the official cut-off team t-shirt??"

"That's right. We used to have the sleeveless team jerseys. And underneath it, we used to throw on a long-sleeve sweat shirt in matching team colors. Same thing all those MTV generation kids are wearing right now."

"At least baseball hats haven't changed much."

"That baseball caps, sonny. And you are correct that they haven't changed much. The old pillbox style with the parallel lines circling the cap came back in style. Guess today's hip, young owners are feeling nostalgic for yesteryear. Even built a stadium or two that's a throwback to Wrigley, Fenway, or Ebbets Field. Think the new ones are called Camden Yards and Coors Field, or something like that."

"Enough of the bittersweet longings," Trebor interjected. "Let's go see a movie. How about *Gone with the Wind*?"

"I was thinking more along the lines of *Terminator 14*, but your selection is fine," replied Hack. "Can you drive? My turbo-charged Corvette is in the shop."

"That's fine. My vintage '34 Ford is purring like a pussy cat."

A View from the Stands

LEARNING TO SCORE

I have discovered, in twenty years of moving around a ballpark, that the knowledge of the game is usually in inverse proportion to the price of the seats.
    Bill Veeck, former White Sox owner

❝ This is supposed to keep me interested in the ball game?" Mrs. Ima Bigfan asked her husband sarcastically. "I've got no clue what all these numbers and abbreviations mean. I think I'll make a hot dog and beer run."

Does the old "6-4-3 DP" leave you feeling down? Don't even know what it is?

No, it's not the periodic chart's atomic composition for infield dirt. It's baseball's way of saying the batter grounded into a short-to-second-to-first double play.

As befuddled as Mrs. Bigfan? Frustrated when your spouse cops an attitude because you don't understand the "S 1-4" play? Does computing a slugging percentage leave you dazed and confused?

"Why do I have to learn these stupid symbols and silly stats anyway?? I just like it when the guy charges out to the pitcher's box swinging the bat," added Mrs. Bigfan.

"That's a pitcher's mound, and that guy is the batter," Mr. Bigfan corrected. "And those brawls have nothing to do with the sport."

"It's more exciting than keeping score," Mrs. Bigfan shot back. "Bob the Beerman, could you explain to me what all these hieroglyphics mean?"

A Season with Bob the Beerman

"I'd be happy to, Mrs. Bigfan," I answered. "After all, that's part of my job, making sure everyone enjoys their stay at the ballpark."

With that, I dropped my case of beer and load of peanuts in the aisle next to Mrs. Bigfan's seat, and began to tell her about the facts of life. From a die-hard baseball fan's perspective.

"Let's see. First, all the players' positions are numbered," I started. "The pitcher is one, catcher is two, first baseman three and so on around the field. Now that's separate from the uniform number each wears, and it isn't reflective of their number of home runs, innings pitched, or runs scored. And there's no correlation between position number, number in the batting order, or number of millions in their contracts. Got that."

"I think so," Mrs. Bigfan answered hesitantly. "Keep going."

"So, if the second batter, playing left field and wearing number nine, grounds out third to first, you have . . ." I continued before being suddenly interrupted by Mrs. Bigfan.

"You have '2nd-7-#9 — GO 5-3' which means he's probably batting about .202 and making $2.2 million," answered Mrs. Bigfan.

"I think you're getting the idea, kind of," I replied with bewilderment. "Now let's move on to the letter symbols used in scoring and in the box scores."

"I'm all set."

"That's what I was afraid of," I countered. "Think of all these abbreviations I'll be giving you as shorthand for a menu. To start, there's 'LOB' which stands for 'low on beer.' The more times a team is LOB during the course of a game, the more it affects their play. And then there's 'BA' which means 'bad attitude.' The greater the number of LOB, the higher the BA, and the worse the team plays."

"I know what you mean," added Mrs. Bigfan. "Every time my husband's softball team gets LOB, then their BA goes sky high."

"Exactly. And when a team has quite a few LOB, then the 'SB - or sodas bought' goes up also. Pitchers and catchers don't like when there are a high number of SB's because then they are responsible for the SB's. Now on to the main course."

"Bob the Beerman, you're making everything so clear. I wish

119

my husband would have used a food analogy every time he'd attempt to teach me how to score," Mrs. Bigfan said.

"It's time to think about ballplayers' favorite foods, and you'll have this down in no time," I said, as Mr. Bigfan rolled his eyes at me in disbelief. "For appetizers, there's 'E' for 'enchilada,' with 'ERA -extra-raw avocado.' This is a favorite between inning snack for the players. The two move in opposite directions. The more E's, the smaller the ERA. Don't quite understand the blend there, but that's the way some stat man cooked those two up.

"And for the entrees, there are 'CS' for 'cold steaks' and 'SF' for 'stale fish.' The more CS by the boys in the dugout, the fewer the SF's. Pretty simple, steak or fish. Of course, you can't forget the 'HR' meaning 'hot rolls.' Some players load up with as many HR's as possible during the game. They throw both the steak and fish on them. Usually lots of HR's mean the hitters feasted off of the pitcher's steak and fish."

"I think I smell the fish all the way up here," quipped Mr. Bigfan. "But keep up the good work, Bob. My wife is learning a lot."

So I continued on with my lessons.

"Some players have many 'AB' or 'all-beef' meals. These are usually the best hitters and they have a high number of AB's. And other players prefer 'NP' or 'no-potatoes.' Pitchers typically have high NP's.

"Finally after eating all this in the dugout during the game, some players have 'BB' for 'bad breath.' Others have some 'RBI' or 'really bad indigestion.' Pitchers hate BB's and RBI's. Batters love them. There was even one player who had 12 episodes of RBI's in one game."

"That can be miserable," Mrs. Bigfan remarked. "I used to get a RBI every time my husband tried to teach me to score. Thanks for making things so easy to understand, Bob!"

"Anytime, Mrs. Bigfan," I replied. "And at some other game, I'll give you my theories on cooking."

STRETCHING

Games played with a ball, and others of that nature, are too violent for the body and stamp no character on the mind."
    Thomas Jefferson, third U.S. President and writer of the
    Declaration of Independence

Some people go to the ballpark early to watch batting practice. Other first arrivers come to watch people. Autograph hounds wait for the gates to open. And some just want to beat the traffic.

I time my entrance with the players' emergence from the locker rooms for warm-up exercises.

Baseball players limbering up, now there's a paradox.

I have never been able to figure out why they need to loosen up before a contest. Most of the ballplayers gather moss standing in the field waiting for a ball to be hit their way.

Yet, this odd, pre-game ritual has the players twisting and turning, bending and reaching, stretching and sweating. Ok, delete sweating from the list. It's like going through a powder puff version of boot camp, with their manager as drill sergeant.

I can hear the manager barking orders. "Give me twenty-five push-ups, on the double!"

I can see the players' response. Three leisurely roll over onto their beer bellies and bury their sleepy heads into their arms. Two others belch in unison as they sit down on the grass. Another adjusts his protective cup. Only one does the push-ups. The guy with the Hanes underwear commercial.

If only one of twenty-five players feel it's important, why bother to do it?

A View from the Stands

Two reasons cross my mind.

The first is that the team's manager and coaches need to fill time somehow, to make it look like the players and themselves actually put in an eight-hour day at their office, the ballpark.

The second is that the players just like putting on a show for all those early birds. It's kind of like seeing the zoo animals after a nap, as they move around in a daze, trying to stretch and shake out the sleep cobwebs. Seeing the players attempt calisthenics is like watching stupid pet tricks. Only the pets are more limber.

The second reason is my top choice. After all, we're talking baseball here, the only major sport to be played in summer's midday heat. That's because there's not enough activity to make anyone perspire despite the temperatures in the 80's.

Take football.

Lots of hitting, tackling. Players covered with bumps and bruises. Forty pounds of equipment worn. That's why it's conducted in autumn's cool weather. They need warm-up exercises.

Take basketball.

Players running, jumping, leaping. Up and down the court. These guys participate in a virtual decathlon every day. They need pre-game stretching.

And take baseball.

The first baseman strolls twenty feet from the shade of the dugout to his position. He doesn't move from that spot until three outs are recorded. Occasionally, he will be forced to trot those five feet to the first base bag to receive a throw from another infielder. More often, he just stands there "adjusting" himself. Does he need to loosen up before the game?

How about the catcher? He just gets comfortable in the dirt behind home plate, and plays toss with the pitcher. Does he need to stretch? As a seven-year old, I don't recall my mother saying, "Little Beercan, make sure you loosen-up before playing in the dirt."

The the last time I looked, the grass had grown to knee level around the outfielders.

And some of the big league pitchers could double as sumo wrestlers in the off-season. These guys are too large to stretch. But it's fun watching them try.

Remember, these aren't athletes, they're baseball players.

A Season with Bob the Beerman

ARMCHAIR GUIDE TO TELEVISED BASEBALL

TV Must Go ... or Baseball Will.
  1952 cover statement, *Baseball* magazine

Everything in today's modern life has become increasingly complicated. Like that sentence. And like popcorn. Who roasts it over an open campfire anymore?

Nowadays, it's nuclear-ready. You have to pull various rip cords on the flat, synthetic package, prop it THIS SIDE UP in the radiation oven, and program a four-step integrated cooking cycle into the microwave.

And when the smoke alarm siren screams, is that the key it's ready for consumption? Of course not, not in the complex, high-tech times we live. Next, it's shake the container VIGOROUSLY! to distribute the salt and butter by-products. Then carefully open the bag by tugging at opposite corners. CAUTION SHOULD BE USED AS STEAM IS EMITTED DURING THE OPENING PROCESS.

Is this technique also used on ballpark popcorn? Or is it for the home version only?

If reclining on the family room couch with the remote control in hand, you better get accustomed to this method of preparing the popcorn.

Nothing is easy anymore.

Including watching baseball on television.

Five hundred stations, satellite dishes, all the major league games - half broadcast on multi-lingual channels, two dozen

A View from the Stands

minor league telecasts, old-timers' games, little league contests from the Far East.

The typical fan of a generation ago now must become a savvy viewer. With this in mind, there are certain keys to watching televised baseball.

* Never, ever, ever, watch the pre-game shows. The game itself will be three-plus hours. Do you want to suffer severe brain damage by tacking another thirty minutes on top of those hours of mind-numbing non-action?

Besides, twenty-four minutes of the warm-up show are filled with automobile and beer commercials. Mostly for sleek sports cars and upscale beers. Makes you feel pretty depressed because you drive a '67 VW Microbus and drink beer that cost $4.49 a case.

* Watch as many games as possible in one sitting. Give the clicker a work-out. Build those thumb and wrist muscles. Channel surfing is encouraged. This will minimize the chance of falling asleep on the couch and spilling beer into your lap while locked into the world's least exciting baseball game.

* Always crank up the volume whenever a play-by-play announcer goes, "A TOWERING FLY BALL! BACK! BACK! BACK! BACK! IT'S OUTTTA HEEERE!!!!" It's guaranteed to get the ear drums ringing, the heart pumping, and the eyelids opening.

It's also a good reminder to restock the refrigerator with favorite foods and beverages. Last time something eventful happened after a player hit a home run was back in '56. That day, the next batter hit the ball out of the infield.

* Immediately turn to another network when an announcer's face appears on the TV screen. Studies have proven that staring at these sportscasters for more than five seconds will turn the viewer to stone.

Be aware of the two types of these talking heads.

The first is the studio stud, with the plastic face and Brill Creme hair. Any exposed flame within one hundred feet will ignite him.

The second is the ex-jock. He's the antithesis to Scotchgard Head. Overweight from too much beer and with a permanent case of hat hair, he epitomizes the former athlete look.

* Turn off the TV and tune in the game on the radio if the telecasters don't give the score within the first ten minutes of watching. These mouths that roared on the television tube will talk your ear off on a wide variety of totally irrelevant topics. From hemorrhoids to hernias, clogged toilets to clogged arteries, the old neighbor lady to the old Edsel which was his very first car, every subject is open for discussion. Except the score.

Who's winning the ball game? With these broadcasters, you'll become intimately acquainted with each and every resident of their Hicksboro Hometown before you hear the score. At least on the radio, the announcers need to be much more descriptive in the call of the action. Just pray that they are.

* Finally, when there's a tight-angled camera shot of a player scratching his privates or picking his butt, that's your hint to visit the bathroom. While there, remember to floss to remove the junk food from between the teeth.

And on the way back to the den, make sure the next bag of popcorn isn't over-radiated. Set it in front of the television. That will pop those uncooked kernels. And cook those unnecessary brain cells.

Somehow, the gray-matter functioned better when life was simpler and there was only baseball books to set eyes upon.

A View from the Stands

So, You Wanted to be a Beerman?

My only regret in life is that I can't sit in the stands and watch me pitch.
  Bo Belinsky, ex-Angel southpaw

Ever get fed up with the stupid rules and regulations that you're forced to follow in everyday life? Ever wanted to rip-up the Magna Carta or punch your boss in the nose? Ever get the desire to go down the supermarket's "six items or less" express check-out lane with seven things?

If so, you meet the criteria to become a beerman.

You see, as a beer vendor, I come under more public scrutiny than a high-powered politician, like, say, the President. And I have to answer to a higher authority.

I'm responsible to those white-collar business executives in big office towers who operate the food and concession services at the ballparks. They produce useful memoranda on burning issues, such as the proper way to don the uniform cap.

An excerpt from one:

The hat must be worn evenly on the top of head, with bill forward. The insignia on the hat cannot be obscured, and no article of material may be worn under the cap. This includes bandanas, headbands, and babushkas.

Those are the actual words on page ninety-six of the authorized vendors' instruction manual. No joke. Each of us was issued one in the pre-season, told it was our Bible, and to learn it cover-to-cover. I don't know about you, but I personally don't know

A Season with Bob the Beerman

many people who have actually read the entire King James Version.

The suits in the management suites are simply following the edicts of the elected officials in each city that oversee the stadium's operations. It's these local government types, like the Deputy-Mayor in-charge-of the Mayor's Deputies, who sit around and think of the various mandates required in order to sell beer at a ball game.

Like ID-ing anyone who appears to be under forty.

That's a lose-lose proposition. If I don't ask for proof of age for someone who's obviously over forty, they're insulted.

"What's the matter, do I look that old," is the typical comment from them. I've heard it many times. Can't someone be more creative?

And if I ask for identification from a person who appears to be thirty-eight, he's bothered that he has to fish out the driver's license. And he'll be further annoyed when I give the news there's a two-beer limit per ID and he won't be able to buy for the entire group.

Chances are, because of the inconvenience factor, they won't be repeat purchasers.

HEY! GUYS IN SUITS AND GOVERNMENT OFFICIALS, WAKE UP! REPEAT BUYERS MEAN ADDITIONAL SALES REVENUE!!!

I wonder how Mr. Deputy-Mayor would like it if his favorite lunchtime cafe suddenly stopped providing preferential treatment on crowded afternoons? Will he continue to frequent that establishment?

Like Mr. Deputy-Mayor's customary restaurant, I'll develop regular patrons during the course of a long season, or even a longer game. And I'm required to ID them for each transaction.

So, suppose the season ticket holder has three beers a game. And there are eighty-one home contests a year. I'm required to check his driver's license two hundred forty-three times during the course of the season. Not only do I know his age, I know his middle initial, where he lives, his wife's name - including all his ex's, his dog's name, what type of car he drives, and how the kids are doing in school. But I still have to check his ID.

A View from the Stands

HEY! GUYS IN SUITS AND GOVERNMENT OFFICIALS, WAKE UP! TIME IS MONEY! THE MORE TIME WASTED WAITING FOR REGULAR CUSTOMERS TO PRODUCE PROPER PAPERWORK MEANS LESS TIME RINGING UP SALES REVENUE!

Where I do business is also controlled. Beer vendors can only sell in the stands. So, if you approach one of us on the concourse en route to you seat, you better not try to buy anything. If you do, one of the Deputy-Mayors' assistants will jump out of a hidden trash receptacle, throw a penalty flag, and issue a citation for improper use of a beerman.

And I'll be slapped with a summons for operating a business in an illegal zone. Must be cutting into the cotton candy sales on the concourse.

HEY! GUYS IN SUITS AND GOVERNMENT OFFICIALS, WAKE UP! EVER HEAR OF THE SHERMAN ANTITRUST ACT PROHIBITING THE RESTRAINT OF COMMERCE? NAFTA? GORE-PEROT DEBATE? NO-TRADE ZONES MEAN LESS SALES REVENUE!

Sorry, sir, what's that? You'd like a couple of beers?

May I see an ID please? And as soon as you get to your seats, I'll be happy to sell you two, Mr. Mayor.

WHERE CAN I GET SOME . . . .

A hot dog at the ballpark is better than steak at the Ritz.
Humphrey Bogart

Yesterday, I couldn't find my car keys. Eventually, I found them in the key-and-loose-pocket-change-basket by the door to the garage. Right where they're supposed to be. Only, no one ever puts them there.

The other morning, I couldn't figure out how to get to the convenience store for some emergency milk for my coffee. Now, I drive passed that place probably six times a day. It's just that I never have a need for anything convenient while I'm driving by. But when the pressure was on and I was becoming desperate for that caffeine fix, I drew a blank. For the life of me, I couldn't remember the way there. After ten minutes driving in circles, I just said "forget the coffee brewing at home. I'll get some here at the donut shop."

The same thing happens at the ballpark. Spectators want to know where to get their favorite food or souvenir. And they usually end-up asking Bob. My beerman uniform must bear an eerie resemblance to those of toll booth collectors. After all, I give directions just as often.

People frequently ask me, "Where can I get a program?" That, along with, "Where's the nearest rest room?" and "Where can I buy those souvenir (put any word in here)?"

So I tell them.

"Take the interstate down to the third South Street exit. Make

A View from the Stands

a double U-turn, then a left at the soft pretzel pushcart. It's the fourth window on the right."

Don't worry, I really don't answer in that tone. But it wouldn't make a difference. Most people can't follow directions anyway.

One time, someone asked me where's the elevator to the upper deck. We were a stone's throw away, so I pointed it out and said, "It's thirty feet ahead on the right."

The man took four strides in that direction, then suddenly veered left down a ramp. Were my instructions that bad??

Sometimes, people ask me where they could obtain cigarettes. So I tell them.

"They can be purchased at the Seven-Eleven across the street from the ballpark. None are sold in here."

So the nicotine junkie does an about-face and hustles off to get a pack of smokes. Of course, I wait until he's out of earshot range before announcing that smoking is no longer allowed in the stadium.

Inevitably, fans call me over to ask where one of the other brands of beer is sold.

So I give them directions.

"Make a left out of the parking lot. Follow the cross-town expressway to the Maple exit. Make a left at the first light. It's the second house on the left."

The beer drinkers of the other brand gaze at me quizzically. "The guy that sells the other stuff called in sick tonight," I continue. "And that's where he lives. So I'm your only option. Isn't it great to live in America where you have freedom of choice?"

And a sign of the times. A couple games ago, a person from out-of-town asked if there was an ATM nearby.

So I directed him to it. "You have to go across the boulevard to the Sports Arena. It's next to the ticket offices on the near-side of the building. But re-admittance to the ballpark is only through gate EEE (for those of wide foot and body), which is on the opposite side of this stadium."

Later in the ball game, I saw him re-enter the ball yard. He appeared dazed and tired. So I asked him how my directions were. "Fine," he replied. "Except my ability to retain them is deteriorating. Got so lost, I had to call 911. And to provide assistance, they wanted directions to where I was located."

Hmmm. A stadium 911 service. It may be the new sign of the times. I'll be the switchboard operator. I could direct people to coffee and donuts.

A View from the Stands

REALIGNMENT

Baseball is the only thing besides the paper clip that hasn't changed.
   Bill Veeck, former Chicago White Sox owner

Some people use *Hooked on Phonics* to learn English. I mastered geography through sports. As a young lad growing up, I got directional fever by checking the pro sports standings in the newspaper.

I discovered Montreal was in another country, but was allowed to compete in our national pastime. I found out that Civil War historians were wrong, Atlanta wasn't a Confederate stronghold in the Deep South. It was actually a western outpost for baseball purposes.

The Gateway to the West, St. Louis, was a misnomer. According to the major league's geography instructor, Mr. Baseball, we were talking east here. Next thing, his wife the science teacher, Mrs. Baseball, told me there weren't any Cardinals within five hundred miles of St. Louis.

And poor Ohio. It was both east and west. I found the Cleveland Indians were in the east, but the Cincinnati Reds were in the west. I guess some consider Ohio the Midwest, while others call it Mideast?? But didn't most Indians live in the wild, wild west? And just how close was Cincinnati to the Pacific Ocean, anyway?

No one ever taught me there was an international dateline cutting through Ohio. I always thought the Mississippi River was the dividing line between east and west. Except to baseball people. Please see St. Louis above.

I was happy to find Houston in the west. A team located in the

A Season with Bob the Beerman

Lone Star State conjured up memories of a gunslinging Texas western. Apparently, baseball officials were big fans of the cowboy and indian flicks. They got this one right.

For Chicago, I needed a course in micro-geography. The Cubs were in the east, but the White Sox were in the west. But I thought the Sox played on the south side of town, while the Cubbies were the northsiders. Not even a Windy City native could explain the logic there.

Then there was Milwaukee. The Brewers moved from Seattle (remember the Pilots?) and were switched from west to east. But last time I checked, Milwaukee was still farther west than Chicago.

And what if Yankees' owner George Steinbrenner isn't blowing smoke and moves the Bronx Bombers across the river to New Jersey?

To New Yorkers, which the baseball demagogues are, anything across the Hudson is the west coast.

Fortunately, when the Dodgers escaped Brooklyn for Los Angeles and the Giants moved to San Francisco from New York, there weren't two divisions. Had there been, they'd still be playing in the east.

Or was that west?

Hope you don't ever need to ask a baseball official for directions.

P.S. - Good luck with realignment. You'll see the world in a whole different perspective.

A View from the Stands

MALFUNCTIONS

A wise man once said a baseball takes funny bounces.
Bob Gibson, St. Louis Cardinal Hall of Fame pitcher

Progress is good, or so they say. Ever wonder who "they" is? Must be the people who manufacture the devices that generate progress. Every time I look, one of these evolutionary gadgets that will make our lives better seems to self-destruct at the most inopportune time.

Like the electronic scoreboard at the ballpark.

Through the first seven innings or three quarters, the high-tech-computer-driven-voice-activated message board runs like a finely tuned Swiss watch not bought on the streets of New York City.

That's until a twelve-run inning late in the contest, or a game-deciding field goal attempt. The fourteen-story, thirty-eight-million-dollar-high-tech wonder which-can-double-for-an-amusement-park then goes haywire.

At Bat becomes %}{LJK~|g%A.

The score shows V-3&3/4 h-NaCl+H20.

And the clock reads 2 :I[]L8.

The big screen DiamondVision can no longer present the *Game of the Week* highlights, nor replays of the controversial calls the umpires blew. The officials don't mind this a bit.

Test patterns will usually materialize. Other times, a scrambled spectrum of colors appear. Viewing these must be what it's like looking at me on a bad hair day.

At not only does it happen during the contest's crucial moments, but only on nationally televised games as well. To cover their butts, the sportscasters immediately advise that the scoreboard has short circuited and that the "Viewers will have to bear with us in describing the action on the field due to the scoreboard's electronic difficulties."

Another excuse for a poorly-announced game.

It also makes the home team and the city appear to the televised audience as cheap dweebs who aren't willing to fork-out the cash to get a fully-functional, state-of-the-art scoreboard.

The team is worth hundreds of millions, but Mr. Tightwad Owner won't spring for a new message board. The municipal officials see millions of dollars pumped into the local economy during each game day, but won't tip the bucket for an improved electronic board system.

Look at Wrigley Field in Chicago and Fenway Park in Boston. Two very wealthy teams. Two very old scoreboards. So dated that they're referred to as venerable. That's just a noble-sounding word to mean ancient.

These two scoreboards were built before micro-chips, radio tubes, and electricity. They're operated with elbow grease. A old man, along with two over-sized rodents, works inside each of these. The inning-by-inning results for all the major league games are posted by hand. And they never malfunction. And they'll never be replaced even though each ownership is loaded with money.

I guess that's understandable.

Before I was rich and famous, I was relieved of numerous jobs. Now that I'm generating big dollars for my employers, they don't want to supplant me with something more modern.

THE END OF A LOVE AFFAIR

It breaks your heart. It is designed to break your heart. The game begins in the spring, when everything else begins again, and it blossoms in the summer, filling the afternoons and evenings, and then as soon as the chill rains come, it stops and leaves you to face the fall alone.
                    Bart Giamatti, the late baseball commissioner

As the long shadows of autumn create a void once filled with summertime's warmth and liveliness, a metamorphosis of the heart occurs. Gone is the passion of the endless summer love, replaced by the wild lust of one-night stands.

What started as a casual interest at a near-tropical locale blossomed through springtime into a nurturing courtship. Warm zephyrs against the face began to fill the bloodstream. The uncertainty of the initial contact transformed into a common understanding, a mutual trust.

Each passing day, the attachment deepened. Arising in the morning, it was the first thing greeted. Sharing a mug of home ground coffee over breakfast, it received undivided attention. So often, thoughts and dreams permeated the waking hours. Soon each was spellbound with sensations new and compelling.

And when separated by travel, daily contact was still maintained. Often numerous times each day. Hotel chocolates on a satin pillow case were no substitutes for an afternoon lunch at the park. Though out of sight, never out of mind.

A Season with Bob the Beerman

As the return date neared, the excitement mounted within. With each renewal, the involvement intensified. The warm summer evenings at home between business trips were filled with the pleasures of companionship. It was an everlasting bond.

But as the first tinges of crisp autumn air displaced the glorious days of sun and shade and summer flowers, so too was the fulfillment of the romance.

Blown into town with the fall's damn foul winds was a brashly seductive item. Sporting a physique as chiseled as the here-I-am attitude, the intrigue was too great.

It was only for a weekend, never more. As the mercury dropped outdoors, the fire burned inside.

It was a snapshot in time. One kept forever in the mind's photo album, unsure if it would ever be re-created.

Yet, as the compost pile grew with the fallen leaves, so to did the collection of erogenous encounters. Every fortnight, it was a new spice and a different taste, and always just weekend activities. Each episode was sordidly sensuous, filled with untethered desire.

Tomorrow, the moment would be gone with the crack of the new workweek against autumn's steel-gray skies.

The summer love affair with baseball had been replaced with the one-night stands of football.

A View from the Stands

About the Authors

Both Bobs grew up back east in Pennsylvania and graduated from Lehigh University, though they did not know one another. While in school, Bob was the sports director of the Lehigh radio network before joining IBM's World Trade Corporation. He proceeded to obtain a MBA in marketing while working there.

The other Bob was a sports writer for The Globe-Times before moving to New York, where he earned a MBA in finance from Fordham University and accepted a position at the Wall Street firm Salomon Brothers.

As a broadcaster, writer, or spectator, the two Bobs have been to 112 different stadiums and arenas on two continents.

The two Bobs met in Denver at the Colorado Rockies' opening day baseball game in April, 1992.

Each presently lives in Boulder, Colorado. They write, perform, entertain, and create, either individually or as one.

Be sure to tell your friends about
A View from the Stands – A Season with Bob the Beerman

Or better yet, buy them a copy using the handy order form / emergency-coffee-table-beer-coaster below. It's the perfect gift for birthdays, Father's Day, holidays and the All-Star Game break (a semi-religious holiday for Bob the Beerman).

Along with the form send a check or money order for $9.95 per book, plus $2.00 shipping for the first book (but only 75¢ shipping for each additional book). Sorry, the post office requires the shipping charges (Bob tried mailing them without postage, but wasn't very successful).

Send your check or money order (no COD's or cash please) to:

> Successful Concepts
> Publishing Dept.
> P.O. Box 3266
> Boulder, CO 80307-3266

Make your check out to "Successful Concepts"

Price valid only in USA. Ground shipping may take three to four weeks.

To get more *Views* from Bob and Bob, or for more book information, write to the above address, or call (303) 499-5926. Outside the 303 area code, call 1-800-FULL MUG (1-800-385-5684).

- - - ✂ -

Yes! Send me ____ copies of *A View from the Stands — A Season with Bob the Beerman* at the price of only $9.95 per copy (plus $2.00 shipping for the first copy and 75¢ for each additional copy). I've enclosed a check/money order for $_____.

Please print clearly

Name _____

Address _____

City/State/ZIP _____

Send this form plus your check or money order to:

Successful Concepts, Pub. Dept., P.O. Box 3266, Boulder, CO 80307-3266